# Pebbles of Joy

A BOOK OF INSPIRATION

*Wishing you peace, love, hope & joy!*

*MaryZabderRoss*

**MARY ZABDER ROSS**

Copyright © 2015 by Mary Zabder Ross

All rights reserved. No part of this publication may be reproduced, stored in a retrieval system, or transmitted, in any form or by any means, electronic, mechanical, photocopying, recording, or otherwise, without the written prior permission of the publisher.

The author of this book does not dispense medical advice nor prescribe the use of any technique as a form of treatment for physical, emotional, or medical problems without the advice of a physician, either directly or indirectly. The intent of the author is only to offer information of a general nature to help you in your quest for emotional, physical, and spiritual well-being. In the event you use any of the information in this book for yourself, the author assumes no responsibility for your actions.

ISBN 978-0-9948303-0-2
Author photo by
GV Ventures Photography
Cover photo by GV Ventures Photography
Cover graphics by Amanda Rea
Cover layout by Iryna Spica
Typeset in *Celestia* at SpicaBookDesign

Printed in Canada
by Printorium Bookworks / Island Blue, Victoria B.C.

# Dedication

This book is dedicated to my wonderful mother, father, and husband. Without their love and support this could never have come to be.

# Acknowledgments

Although a story is written by one, a book is created by many. Consequently, I have many people to thank.

A heartfelt thank you to everyone who contributed to this effort in ways both great and small. Michelle Mahood, Sharon Lehman, and Dr. Brian Taylor, thank you for generously agreeing to review my manuscript. You provided me with invaluable feedback and I am immensely appreciative of the time and effort you committed to this endeavour.

To all my wonderful family and friends, I am truly grateful. Your genuine interest and enthusiasm in this adventure ensured that the fire within me kept burning brightly.

To my husband, Earl Ross. You are, and have always been, my greatest champion. Your encouragement and support have remained steadfast and unwavering throughout this entire process. You believed in me from the beginning, never once losing faith in my abilities, even when mine faltered. Because there are no words that could possibly express my appreciation, I will simply say, I love you.

A very special thank you to my niece Nadine Zabder and her partner Benjamin Hoy. You enhanced and enriched this entire experience with selfless offerings of your time, kind words, knowledge, and expertise.

Thank you Iryna Spica from SpicaBookDesign and Craig Shemilt from Island Blue Printing for turning a manuscript into the book that I had envisioned.

May all the joy that everyone has blessed me with return to you many times multiplied. I know that the light shining through all of our efforts is that of the Divine. May we all remember to be grateful.

# Table of Contents

Acknowledgments ............................. v
Foreword  ................................. ix
Introduction............................... xiii

| | | |
|---|---|---|
| *Chapter 1* | Once Upon a Time................. 1 |
| *Chapter 2* | Spinning Straw into Gold .......... 5 |
| *Chapter 3* | Be Aware of the Wolf.............. 11 |
| *Chapter 4* | I Think I Can.................... 17 |
| *Chapter 5* | A Tale of Two Stories ............. 23 |
| *Chapter 6* | The Lesson ...................... 29 |
| *Chapter 7* | Living Well...................... 35 |
| *Chapter 8* | Knocking on Heavens Door ....... 45 |
| *Chapter 9* | The Price of Magic................ 53 |
| *Chapter 10* | A Whole New World.............. 65 |
| *Chapter 11* | The Heart of Happiness ........... 75 |

| | | |
|---|---|---|
| *Chapter 12* | The Best Present | 81 |
| *Chapter 13* | Mirror Mirror | 89 |
| *Chapter 14* | Small Things Do Make a Big Difference | 97 |
| *Chapter 15* | Finding Love | 103 |
| *Chapter 16* | Three Wishes | 109 |
| *Chapter 17* | A Time For Change | 117 |
| *Chapter 18* | Some Things are Not Meant to Disappear | 127 |
| *Chapter 19* | A Never Ending Story | 133 |

# Foreword

*E*arly in my career as an academic teaching surgeon, I was fortunate to work closely with Mary Zabder Ross on the surgical wards, and together we cared for many seriously ill patients. I was struck by her dedication, passion for her patients, and her unwavering loyalty to them. When Mary called and said she was worried about a patient, I paid attention….she was seldom wrong. After I moved to another hospital, our paths seldom crossed. Then one day, three months after I retired, we met again; this time in a retirement home where I was performing, playing Canadian folk music for the residents of the home, and she had by chance been visiting there with a friend. My passion for music had led me down this new path, and Mary's passion for writing became clear as we discussed our current lives and our new perspectives. From this "chance" meeting came the offer for me to read

"Pebbles of Joy" during its final stages of development. It was clear to me that Mary's life experiences and her observations from a dedicated career in nursing were the basis for the examples in this book.

I wish I had been motivated or told to read a book like "Pebbles of Joy" early in my career. Surgeons are expected primarily to read scientific articles about technical procedures and apply these ideas to their practices. However, very often in my profession I would find myself dwelling on the negative aspects, the mistakes, and the failures….. and the resulting feelings of frustration and uncertainty were sometimes hard to overcome. "Pebbles of Joy" teaches us the importance of viewing events of our life from a positive perspective. It reminds us that knowledge is gained from all of our life experiences. By focusing on the positive we can in fact abandon our frustrations and negativity and thus feel more energized, uplifted, and joyful.

As I have grown older, I have also learned the value of being reflective and grateful by saying a prayer of gratitude each day on my morning walk with my dog. The pause taken to do this simple act makes me realize how fortunate I have been in life; it makes me realize that the worries of the day are

## Foreword

far less of an issue in the face of all that is good and I cannot help but feel grateful. The feelings of peace, satisfaction, and motivation that flow from this simple act are almost palpable. To my delight, this very example was addressed in this book.

"Pebbles of Joy" will teach you the simple but energizing values that come from reflection, from being grateful, from helping others, and from dealing with negative issues in a proactive way. I hope your eyes and minds will be opened just as much as mine were.

Dr. Brian Taylor

# Introduction

The Universe is patient. It grants us an eternity to live up to our potential. Do we really want to wait that long? The time to start making our incredible discoveries is now. Enlightenment doesn't happen overnight. The sooner we get started, the sooner we can become the light of joy in this world.

Life does not come with instructions. That's just as well, as half of the population wouldn't bother to read them, the rest of us might pore over every word and still we would be left wondering. I don't know if we were meant to unravel all of life's mysteries, however, that thought should not stop us from trying.

I believe that we do have control over our destiny. Free will means exactly that. We are free to choose as we wish. I also believe that, although we are helped by the Divine, it is our hand that writes the script for each incarnation. We choose the adventures that we desire most. We also choose experiences that we will learn the most from. We can act out our story as planned, or we can alter it. The choice is ours.

But how do we go about creating the best life story possible? How can we transcend adversity? Where do we find happiness? Why do we search for love? What is the secret to living a life of abundance? We may have forgotten, but the answer to every one of these questions lies somewhere within us. We just need to be reminded of all that we already know. For this, we need each other. By listening to and by welcoming each other into our stories, no one will be left in darkness.

Some of us may not be destined to do great things, but to paraphrase Mother Teresa, we can at least do something small and we can do it with great love. In my experience, it is often the smallest things that can make the biggest difference.

Providing comfort while caring for patients is what I have always loved most about my position as a registered nurse. With increasing frequency, however, I found myself thinking that there had to be a better way to help people feel happier and healthier. Eventually I knew that the time had come to do something different. Something more. Something sooner. Something, before the damage was done.

I can understand how difficult it is to accomplish even the simplest task when we are at our lowest; even if someone throws us a life line, we don't have the strength to reach for it. Maybe a well-meaning family member or friend will try to force feed us with a cornucopia of good will, however, we can't seem to stomach even the best of intentions. Unfortunately, we end up rejecting both the messenger and the sound advice. With that in mind, it occurred to me that life could be so much better if we could learn how to stay happy and healthy in the first place. Thus, the idea to create Pebbles of Joy was born.

Not feeling particularly healthy, wealthy, or happy? Do not despair. Regardless of where you are on the prosperity scale, this book is written for you. The only prerequisite is to have an open mind and a genuine desire for a more joyful and fulfilling life. The exercises are designed to be rejuvenating and uplifting, yet will require nothing more than turning a page. The diet? Simply an abundance of food for thought that anyone can partake in, be nourished by, and hopefully, truly enjoy.

We toss a little pebble into the still waters of a clear pond and we know that it will only make a tiny splash. Yet, if we wait patiently, we will see the ripples extending far and wide in ever expanding circles. I'm offering these little pebbles of joy that I have gathered so that you may use them in this very big pond of life. Believing in the power of the ripple effect, my hope is that our combined joy will spread far and wide.

*The world is in need of more joy.*
*It is up to you and me to fill that need.*

## Chapter 1

# Once Upon a Time

> "Everything is possible for the
> one who believes."
>
> MARK 9:23

  *E*veryone has a story to tell. One will be full of love and laughter, another will sag beneath the weight of misery and sorrow. Our life story will hold a certain degree of both extremes, hopefully far more joy than grief. We cannot change what has happened in the past, but if we believe, we may be certain that our future can be joyous, amazing, and wonderful.

  The most cherished memory I have of my mother is how, with heartfelt sincerity and love, she would always wish me the best of everything. My father, a diamond in the rough, inspired me to strive to be the best that I could be. I have come to believe that the way for us to experience the best of everything and to live up to our potential is by awakening and expanding the joy and love within our hearts.

We all believe in different things. Some of our beliefs we can be certain of. Others we cannot. You may agree with some of my beliefs, while others you may doubt, or perhaps completely disagree with. You are absolutely free to choose as you will. I only ask that you embrace what expands and uplifts you, and simply let go of that which does not.

The first secret in Dr. Wayne Dyer's *10 Secrets for Success and Inner Peace*, is to "have a mind that is open to everything and attached to nothing." Consider adopting this approach when presented with new ideas and different ways of thinking. It will always serve you well. Remember, when something rubs us the wrong way, there may be either long standing ingrained beliefs, or very personal experiences at the root of our reaction. Surprisingly, some of the things which we guard closely may not be entirely correct, or even true. Examining the point in question a little closer, especially from a different perspective, could be to our benefit, healing, and growth. By keeping "a mind that is open to everything and attached to nothing," we will have taken the first and most important step toward restoring peace, joy and freedom in our hearts and minds. This is what I wish for everyone!

We are the authors of our life story. How the story unfolds, and how it ends, is up to us. May everyone's story begin with "once upon a time," and end "happily ever after."

## Chapter 2
# Spinning Straw into Gold

"Be the change you wish
to see in the world."
MAHATMA GANDHI

*S*tory telling. Just as the binding joins the pages of a book, it is the magic that weaves an invisible thread and gathers us together as one. Everywhere on this beautiful planet we have been passionately sharing our stories since the beginning of time. Sometimes they will be that which legends are made of. Others times, the lessons and morals will be written into myths and parables and songs. When imagination and dreams combine, they create timeless treasures. Stories help to define us. Some create laughter, some create tears. Most incredible of all however, are the stories that contain carefully preserved secrets. We find them hidden within the pages of books both old and new, waiting to enlighten and expand us.

At first glance, these tales may appear to be nothing more than a pleasant and interesting distraction. When we look closer however, we unravel the mysteries written in the words and lines. Suddenly, wondrous truths to live by shall be revealed.

Rich or poor, saint or sinner, strong or weak, there is a law that applies to every person on this planet. This law is shaping your life story whether you are aware of it or not. It discriminates against no one. It is impartial and it is always in effect. It is, of course, the Law of Attraction.

For centuries philosophers, scholars, and modern day thinkers have been teaching and writing about this law. Why has it remained such a mystery? Have we not been listening? What are we failing to see? Maybe, we are listening but not fully understanding. Sometimes it just takes the right book to open our hearts and our minds, the right story to remind us of all that we have forgotten.

What exactly is this mysterious Law of Attraction? I believe it is the answer to many of our questions about how life works. It is the means by which we create and alter our life stories, and it is what allows us to spin straw into gold.

The Law of Attraction is the name given to the process of how we draw certain thoughts, people, things and situations into our lives. It is based on the theory that everything in life is made of energy, including our thoughts and feelings. We create our reality by attracting into our lives whatever energies our thoughts and feelings are aligned with. "Like" attracts "like." Thinking and feeling positive thoughts attracts more positive experiences into our life, while feeling and thinking negatively attracts more negativity.

It is by this process that we can create a life of abundance or manifest a life of scarcity; either being the result of our beliefs, thoughts and feelings.

To be clear, the Law of Attraction is not just about thinking positively. The creative process is more complex. We have to believe and feel that we are worthy of good things before good things can come our way. To allow abundance into our life, we cannot remain focused on all that we are lacking. Instead, we must find a way to feel good about what we do have, no matter how little it may be.

When we have a mindset of scarcity we are acting out of fear that there will never be enough. With this kind of thinking, regardless of how much we have, we will always feel that something is missing. Happiness eludes us. However, when our perception is that of abundance, we will feel that our life is truly plentiful even if it may not appear so to others.

The Law of Attraction is not a new concept. It is neither complicated, nor difficult to comprehend, and yet, often times it is not as readily accepted as one might think it would be. Why is there so much resistance to incorporating an idea that requires so little effort and results in such great returns?

Is it because we are creatures of habit? Are we reluctant to accept change even when it is for the better? At best, we may not be particularly happy with our present situation, but it is familiar and tolerable, so we carry on the same old way and claim that everyday life got in the way of fulfilling our dreams. Maybe it's just easier to blame our misfortune on something or someone. By refusing to look inward to expand our awareness and growth, we deny our God-given power. Believing we are impotent, we risk losing ourselves in hopeless misery. When this happens, we may fail to comprehend why abundance eludes us.

If we are immersed in a particular faith from a young age, we may find ourselves reluctant to entertain any thoughts contrary to whatever it is we have been taught. Sadly, our way of thinking has been too often shaped by fear. To consider a new way of thinking, anything that challenges a particular belief of ours will likely be perceived as wrong. Understandably, nobody wants to risk spending eternity in an undesirable location.

By embracing the Laws of Attraction we may worry that we are claiming all power for ourselves, thereby dismissing the need for a "higher power" in our lives. This is perhaps the greatest stumbling block that we might encounter in accepting our role in the creative process.

Admittedly, throughout history humans have acted unspeakably, claiming their abhorrent actions to be God's will. At times, religious views and doctrine have distorted the essence of our Creator. Rather than elevating our collective spirit, unyielding beliefs have torn people, communities, and nations apart. Because of such folly, we can easily understand why some may oppose even hearing the word "God." This is, in part, why I will often choose to refer to our Creator as "the Universe" or "the Divine." Not only do these terms evoke a greater sense of expansiveness, but without the interference of a negative name association my hope is that we can all experience our Creator in a far more favorable light.

Clinging to old beliefs, ones that judge and separate, can be limiting and narrow minded. Incredibly, by opening our minds to a much broader and more inclusive point of view, our perception of the Universe and of each other expands. Suddenly God is not just a one man show keeping score and playing favorites. Instead, the Divine is everywhere, in everyone, and in everything. Our new and expanded beliefs haven't removed God from our lives, rather, now we are far more aware of how every part of our life, and every life for that matter, includes the Divine.

I may never determine exactly what prevents a person from believing in something incredible, but I am here to remind you that The Law of Attraction is playing a huge part in your everyday life. By understanding the role our thoughts play in the creative process we can effectively create a wonderful, happy, and more fulfilling life.

We can dismiss this opportunity for change and we can continue to struggle against the current. Indeed, we can keep asking ourselves, "why me?" Or, we can change our outlook and our stories. With nothing to lose, and everything to gain, why not?

So, let us rewrite our story to be one full of joy. Let us become the change we wish to see in the world, and in the process, let us discover the secret to spinning straw into gold.

# Chapter 3
# Be Aware of the Wolf

"Most of the shadows of this life are caused
by our standing in our own sunshine."

RALPH WALDO EMERSON

*H*appiness means something different for everyone. What brings the most cheer to one person will not always lift the spirits of the next. Regardless, life is simply much better when we are happy. I may not know exactly what brightens your day, but I am quite certain that pain, illness, and scarcity will diminish anyone's joy.

No one would choose any one of these burdens for themselves on purpose, and yet, unknowingly, in many ways we do. Choosing thoughts that are consistently fearful or negative will affect us adversely, eventually putting our mental or physical state out of balance. When this happens we put ourselves at risk for various ailments and disease. If we consider that the majority of all illnesses are precipitated and prolonged by stress, we can then appreciate the immense power and influence that our pattern of thinking has over our physical condition.

Recognizing and being clear about what we don't want is the first step towards ultimately attaining what we do desire. I believe that most of us hope for happiness, good health, and prosperity.

This story has been attributed to the Cherokee, although its origin is difficult to establish. Like most old stories, it has been subject to many retellings. Its message, however, is so brilliant in its simplicity and wisdom that it is worth repeating. Despite any changes, I believe that the story remains true to the intended teaching.

> *One evening a Cherokee elder told his grandson about the battle that goes on inside people. He said, "My son, the battle is between two wolves that live inside us all. One is unhappiness. It is fear, worry, anger, jealousy, self pity, guilt, regret, arrogance, resentment and inferiority. The other is happiness.*

## Be Aware of the Wolf

*It is joy, peace, love, hope, serenity, generosity, humility, kindness, truth, compassion and faith." The grandson thought about this for a minute and then asked his grandfather, "which one wins?" The old Cherokee simply replies, "the one you feed."*

We have to ask ourselves, "How many times did I feed the wrong wolf?" For many, the answer will most likely be, "more often than I should have." Battling the monster that we have been supporting will naturally be a daunting and exhausting task. Instead, we must turn our attention toward the wolf we have neglected, and start nourishing our body and soul with positive and loving thoughts. Meanwhile, hungry and ignored, the wolf of fear and anger, which we are no longer aiding will hopefully seek refuge elsewhere, or better yet, perish altogether.

Our bodies are always responding to what we are thinking, as well as the specific words that we are speaking. What we may not realize is how much our subconscious, and thereby our wellness, is affected by our everyday utterances. Too often, without giving it a second thought, we announce that we are fighting some illness or annoyance. We might be referring to something as basic as the common cold or as serious as cancer. No matter what the ailment, disease, or issue may be, we have to recognize that it takes a great deal of energy to battle anything, especially infirmities of any kind. Since our ultimate goal is to restore peace and harmony to our system, why not declare that we are transcending what ails us, or that we are in the process of reclaiming our health whenever we are not feeling well. Those words alone have a noticeable difference in energy and vibration. Coming from a place of trust, not fear, they tell us a completely different story, one that implies and defines a more favorable and desired outcome.

It bears repeating that our anger, worry, fears, jealousy, self pity, guilt, resentment, and inferiority, are very powerful emotions that are not only undermining our happiness, but in actuality, are largely responsible for making us sick.

I would imagine that most of us can easily appreciate how detrimental stress and negative, or fearful thinking is to our well-being. Who hasn't experienced a time of prolonged tension or intense strain and then in some way, either physically or mentally, suffered as a result?

The way that these negative forces manifest within us might vary widely, but manifest they do. After several decades of being a nurse and bearing witness to the unthinkable, one thing is clear to me; preventing a problem is much easier than the exhaustive effort required to correct one. Our bodies are incredibly crafted, and thus, we shouldn't be breaking down so often, nor should we be in constant need of adjustment and repair. How many parts do we need to replace, reconstruct, or remove, before we ask ourselves, "What is going on here?" It doesn't make sense that at a time when we have so much, that we should find ourselves so lacking. We should all be physically and emotionally thriving, not failing.

The intimate relationship between body and mind is unparalleled. The more we appreciate this connection the better off we will be. There is no mystery here, harmonious thoughts will help keep us healthy, while an accumulation of unhealthy thoughts, such as fear, resentment, anger, and guilt, will perpetuate disease.

Although we all should have quit feeding the wolf of unhappiness a long time ago, it's never to late to stop. However, we cannot fix a problem with the same kind of thinking that contributed it. Perhaps it is time we start thinking differently!

Chapter 4

# I Think I Can

"Whether you think you can or you think you can't, either way you will be right."

HENRY FORD

Sometimes, the hardest thing about getting started is just that, getting started. It doesn't matter what it is that we want to accomplish, often times there is something holding us back. We might have any number of excuses, but the truth is, the most likely obstacle preventing us from moving forward is our thoughts. Now, trusting the fact that you will be right "whether you think you can, or you think you can't" wouldn't it be better to give yourself the benefit of the doubt?

Take, for instance, my hesitation with getting this book started. I had just finished reading, for the second time, *You Can Heal Your Life*, by Louise L. Hay, when all kinds of doubts started to plague me. *You Can Heal Your Life* appeared twice on the New York Times best sellers list with more than 30 million copies sold. This book offers practical, detailed, and extensive advice on how to improve your life. Could I really offer anything more? Anything even remotely comparable?

That is where my story could have ended. All that I had planned to share was about to vanish because of doubt. Rather than let that happen, I changed the direction of my thoughts. Considering that there are millions of books and millions of readers, it was safe to conclude that what connects with one person may not connect with another. Each story has its own flair and ability to inspire. Bingo! "Too much of a good thing" doesn't necessarily apply when it comes to being inspired. We always benefit from anything that uplifts our spirits, and brings us true joy. I suddenly recognized the truth. This is not a competition. My sole purpose in creating this book was to infuse as much joy into everyone's life as possible. With that simple thought, I was happily able to continue on with my story.

Thoughts are very powerful. They will either move us forward or hold us back, nothing else, just our thoughts. We must choose them carefully and wisely. In all that we do or wish to become, our thoughts will be our greatest ally, or our most formidable enemy.

What we choose to think and speak about is going to multiply by the Law of Attraction. To be mindful of what we are focusing on is imperative, especially when things don't go our way. Whenever we get too emotional we can easily lose our focus. Unfortunately, because we are feeling with such intensity, we send out strong negative signals and become powerful magnets for more of what we would rather not have. If you don't believe me, try starting your morning off complaining about everything, and then tell me how much fun you have had come the end of the day.

One of the easiest ways of avoiding this negativity trap, is simply by removing all negative words from our vocabulary. If we are faithful in doing this, we will never again declare that we are having a bad day, because "bad" no longer exists in our list of adjectives. When we start believing that every day is a good day, it becomes our reality sooner than we can imagine.

Make no mistake, this is not to say that our problems are going to miraculously disappear, nor will we instantly become immune to, or exempt from all danger. Difficulties are part of life. They help us to grow. Often, it is because of our toughest challenges, that we learn the most valuable lessons.

I am not advocating that we ignore our problems. Doing that might invite trouble at best, or could be disastrous at worst. Neither am I asking you to pretend everything is perfect when it is not. Instead, I am suggesting that we perceive adversity in a different way. Rather than dismissing the entire day as bad, we must realize that there really is no such thing as a bad day. This slight alteration in thinking allows us to recognize the blessings hidden amongst misfortune. If we can first focus our thoughts on what went well, then we can view the entire day's events from a better perspective. With this approach we are more likely to learn from our difficult experiences rather than feel beaten down by them.

Truthfully, a day is just a day. In essence, it is neither good nor bad. It simply becomes whatever we choose to think it to be.

Perhaps you're thinking that this sounds way too good to be true, maybe even bordering on the absurd. Most likely, that is just your old way of thinking attempting to sabotage an incredible opportunity. Here is your chance to improve every remaining day that you have left on this beautiful planet. I can't imagine why that would not at least be worth a second thought.

The book As We Think, So We Are, is a modern interpretation of James Allen's work originally called As a Man Thinketh. Included is the original text as written in 1902, but since much has changed in the last hundred years, including language, the updated version by Dr. Ruth Miller is more comprehensive. One incredibly powerful statement that is made in the book is, "that the outer conditions of our lives always reflect our inner states, so circumstances don't make us; they reveal us to ourselves." Wow! Now that packs a punch! So what have you been thinking? Don't know? Well, take a good look around you, and within you. Are you happy with what you see and feel? Or are you in need of some improvement? If we are not in a good place, this thought may not be what we want to hear. However, immediately following this essential point Dr. Miller, interpreting Allen's words, states:

> *Of all the beautiful truths that have been restored and brought to light in this age, none will promise you more joy and blessedness in mind and spirit than this--that you are the master of your thoughts, the molder of your character, and the maker and*

*shaper of your condition, your environment, and your destiny. As a being of power, intelligence, and love and the controller of your own thoughts, you hold the key to every situation; you contain within yourself all the means to make yourself and your life what you will.*

How empowering is that! When we decide to take responsibility for our circumstance, we haven't taken a first step toward happiness, we have taken a gigantic leap toward a life of joy. When we stop believing that we are at the mercy of whoever or whatever appears to be tormenting us, then we immediately reclaim our power and begin the process of creating a new life for ourselves.

By recognizing that our inner thoughts create our outer world, we become very mindful of the thoughts we wish to entertain. Now that we understand the power and unlimited potential of our thoughts, we will be better able to choose carefully and wisely. Now, we can rewrite our life story to our liking.

# Chapter 5
# A Tale of Two Stories

"Is the universe friendly?"
ALBERT EINSTEIN??

*L*ife is continuously presenting us with choices. We choose what we think about and what we believe in. We choose the character of our speech, and we choose how we are going react in any given situation. In fact, everything that we do is a matter of choice. Some decisions are inconsequential, while others are monumental. Sometimes we choose wisely, sometimes poorly. Our life story is the sum total of all of our thoughts and resultant choices.

Deciding whether the Universe is friendly or not is an important choice that we all must make. If we don't make this decision consciously, we will do it subconsciously.

## Pebbles of Joy

We live in a complex world. No one is likely to dispute that. Sometimes terrible things happen to good people. Sometimes good things happen to people who act terribly. Life does not always appear to be reasonable, just, or fair. Often we find ourselves struggling to make sense of the incomprehensible. Keep in mind that we do not have the privilege of seeing the picture in its entirety. We have to believe that there is order in the grand scheme of life, and that the Universe is friendly. To believe otherwise is to resign ourselves to a world of chaos and despair.

When we focus on, and do nothing other than complain about the misery and injustice in the world, we are only adding to the problem. We will become part of the solution when we believe in and promote joy, abundance, and dignity for all.

How many times have you seen the following quotation? "Is the universe friendly?" Have you ever wondered about its context? Legend would have us believe that this is how Einstein responded when a reporter asked him what he thought the most important question facing humanity might be. Unfortunately, I could not find any credible source to prove that Einstein actually said, "Is the universe friendly?" Still, it's a very good question; a question that we as individuals must ultimately ask

## A Tale of Two Stories

ourselves. I've chosen to include the remainder of this message, even if it was not truly spoken by him, because it is in keeping with Einstein's desire for world peace and with his wish that every person be treated with dignity. Regardless of who the actual author is, the remainder of the story reads as follows. The writer may be speaking on a grand scale, but it is just as applicable on an individual basis.

> *For if we decide that the universe is an unfriendly place, then we will use our technology, our scientific discoveries and our natural resources to achieve safety and power by creating bigger walls to keep out the unfriendliness and bigger weapons to destroy all that which is unfriendly and I believe that we are getting to a place where technology is powerful enough that we may either completely isolate or destroy ourselves as well in this process.*
>
> *If we decide that the universe is neither friendly nor unfriendly and that God is essentially 'playing dice with the universe,' then we are simply victims to the random toss of the dice and our lives have no real purpose or meaning.*
>
> *But, if we decide that the universe is a friendly place, then we will use our technology, our scientific discoveries and our natural resources to create*

*tools and models for understanding that universe. Because power and safety will come through understanding its workings and its motives.*

Clearly there is only one desirable answer. Do we not all wish to be safe and powerful? Of course we do, but not at the expense of anyone else. Remember, we are not speaking of a power that seeks to oppress, but of a personal power. That same power that gets us out of bed in the morning is just as likely to lift a fellow human out of poverty, and without question, it all begins with one little thought.

We may never completely understand the workings of the Universe, but we can decide that it is friendly, and thus move forward secure, confident, and with joy in our hearts. Remember, you are the author of your story, what you choose to believe in and focus on is going to manifest in your life and become part of your script.

I believe that the Universe is friendly, and that life is meant to be incredible, joyful, and beautiful. For as long as I keep that my primary focus, it will remain my reality. Why would I choose otherwise? Keep in mind that the operative word here is focus. Naturally, some of our experiences in life will be less than pleasant, but even in the most challenging

## A Tale of Two Stories

situations we can still find something positive to reflect upon.

Perhaps there is another very important question we must ask ourselves. That is, is the story that we are telling ourselves true? Are we practicing selective amnesia and forgetting about all the positives in our lives and in the world? Are we focusing solely on the negative aspects of the present or the past? If that is the case, then the story we are telling ourselves is not entirely true, and is not serving us well. We can just as easily acknowledge that although things may not be quite perfect, there is much to be grateful for, and start focusing on what is right in our lives and in our world.

Simply by shifting our thoughts, our entire perspective changes and consequently, the picture upon which we have focused. Whether it be our view of the past, or our interpretation of the present, a transformation will occur, for better or worse, according to our intention. Remember, what we focus on is going to expand and multiply, so let us shine our light on all that is good, and start creating a much happier story and time in which to live.

"It was the best of times, it was the worst of times, it was the age of wisdom, it was the age of foolishness, it was the epoch of belief, it was the epoch of incredulity, it was the season of Light, it was the season of Darkness, it was the spring of hope, it was the winter of despair, we had everything before us, we had nothing before us," so begins the classic, *Tale of Two Cities*, by Charles Dickens.

That we live in a world of duality, as Dickens so eloquently portrays, is undeniable. Sometimes we will find this world beyond incredible, and at other times, almost unbearable. We must remember however, that often times the intensity with which we experience an emotion is directly related to the degree that we have experienced its opposite. Would we really understand the meaning of happiness if we never knew sadness? Would we be as grateful for warmth if we were never cold? Would we so cherish the loving embrace if we never knew the agony of loneliness? Would we appreciate the light if we never experienced darkness? Maybe, but probably not. From this perspective, life doesn't seem quite so harsh, and all of a sudden the Universe is looking a little more friendly.

So, do we choose wisdom or foolishness? Belief or disbelief? Light or darkness? Hope or despair? Ultimately, when we decide that the Universe is friendly or unfriendly, we will have also chosen the best or the worst story to be our own.

## Chapter 6
# The Lesson

"Forgiveness is the fragrance that the violet leaves on the heel that has crushed it."

MARK TWAIN

From the moment we are born until the time of our passing, it seems we are always learning something new. Some lessons are fun and easy. We grasp them quickly. Others are more challenging. They are the lessons that may take a lifetime to master.

Life's first lesson. Breathing. We cannot avoid learning this skill. Our survival depends on it. Fortunately, it comes to us naturally. When times get tough and we find ourselves in a stressful situation, what should we remember to do? That's right. Focus on the very first lesson we ever learned. Just breathe!

At the opposite end of the spectrum lies our final lesson. Letting go. Until we familiarize ourselves with this exercise it will be impossible for us to move on. This task may seem simple enough, but if we tend towards being stubborn, we are really going to struggle with this one.

Our entire life is cleverly sandwiched in between these two lessons. The Universe allows us ample opportunity to practice both breathing and letting go.

So how do we let go of anger, resentment, frustration and anxiety? How do we replace toxic thoughts with serenity and joy? I believe that a delightful little children's story called, *The Bike Lesson*, by Stan and Jan Berenstain can help us with the ultimate act of letting go: forgiveness. But what could a bike lesson possibly have in common with forgiveness? At first glance apparently nothing. When we look closer however, we will see that the story contains a clue to this very important lesson.

For those of you who never had the privilege of enjoying this humorous storybook, it's about a father bear trying to teach his son how to ride a bicycle. Each progressive lesson results in a failed attempt at showing the little cub the correct way to ride a bike.

## The Lesson

Throughout the story, after each lesson and resulting disaster, Father Bear declares, "That is what you should not do," and Small Bear enthusiastically exclaims variations of "thanks Dad, that was a very good lesson for me." The tale ends with Small Bear riding the bike home with a bruised and battered Father Bear sitting on the handlebars.

Before continuing, I must clarify that although I have chosen a lighthearted story to illustrate a point, it is not meant to minimize the seriousness and complexity of forgiveness. I recognize and acknowledge that the transgressions that I have had to let go of pale in comparison to the atrocities that have been endured, overcome and forgiven by others. Indeed, much of this adversity seems far beyond our capacity to even begin to comprehend. By human standards, the ability to forgive grave offenses is nothing short of miraculous. To manifest this amazing grace, another aspect of our nature has to be accessed. That aspect is our authentic selves. The spirit within us will always recognize the truth. Our spirit will remember that we are all equally loved, that we are all one, and that we are all doing the best that we can at any given moment, considering our circumstances.

Therein lies the connection between the bike lesson and forgiveness. Father Bear, although failing miserably, is simply doing the best he can. Keep in mind that in the end, he does at least manage to teach his son what not to do.

Obviously Father Bear's lack of bicycling skills isn't something that would warrant forgiveness, but the reality is, our parents, and those in whom we have placed our trust often fall short in far more crucial ways. As children, and even as adults, we often expect our loved ones to be knowledgeable in many things, to protect us from harm, and above all, to love us unconditionally. It's a tall order that few can completely fulfill. Sadly, there will also be many who won't know how or where to even begin. Naturally, when we are expecting the best from someone and instead receive what appears to be their worst, deep and long lasting wounds may result.

Whether it be anger, resentment or guilt, finding a way to release whatever negativity may be festering within us isn't likely to come easily. If we should hope to truly reclaim our joy we have to stop feeding the wolf of unhappiness. We have to find a way to rid ourselves of these lingering painful thoughts.

When we need to make peace with ourselves or with others, an extremely effective path to forgiveness is to remember that everyone is just doing the best that they can at any given moment. Even if

## The Lesson

we find this hard to believe, we can still give them the benefit of the doubt. This very simple thought never fails to ease my mind and soften my heart. Furthermore, just like riding a bike, once you learn this useful skill, chances are very good that you are not likely to forget it.

This may appear to be an excessively lenient stance to take, especially in the event of serious crimes or heinous acts. It may even give the impression that we are exempting all wrongdoers from taking responsibility for their actions. Not so. Instead, it merely provides a safe and effective means of shifting our focus, so that we may free ourselves from harboring feelings of anger and resentment, neither of which are likely to be conducive to our well-being.

Remember, very few things can ignite our inner rage quicker than being the victim of, or bearing witness to any type of assault, especially that which violates the innocent and vulnerable. It is here that we must be extremely mindful of our thoughts, for if we continue to feed that inner wolf of hate, we risk becoming another reflection of all that we were initially so appalled and outraged by. In other words, we must find a safe and effective way to let go of the angry wolf, before we are consumed by it.

Sometimes, the person we need to forgive most is ourselves. Unresolved guilt is an extremely heavy burden that we need not carry. It is the equivalent of donning an anvil for a hat, and then wondering what is pressing so heavily on our mind and causing the rest of our body to suffer with unexplained pain. By constantly carrying around this heavy weight, what are we accomplishing? Absolutely nothing!

When guilt prompts us to right a wrong, or if it deters us from further wrong doing, then clearly we can see how guilt can be advantageous. Unresolved guilt however, can become an all consuming guilt. This is a pointless and futile emotion, because simply feeling bad is never going to make us or anyone else feel any better.

Without question, resentment and unresolved guilt are extremely detrimental to our happiness and well-being. If we wish to live fuller, freer, and more joyful lives, it is absolutely vital that we find a way to rid ourselves of these toxic thoughts and emotions. How we choose to go about doing this is completely up to us, but we really should find a way to let go of all that does not serve us well, because at the end of the day, when we find a way to forgive, we have found a far better way to live.

# Chapter 7
# Living Well

"If the only prayer you ever say in your entire
life is thank you, it will be enough."

MEISTER ECKHART

*I*f I could capture the essence of happiness and place it in a bottle it would be labelled "Gratitude." As Brother David Steindl-Rast states, "It is not happiness that makes us grateful, but gratefulness that makes us happy."

Never underestimate the power of gratitude. If you wish to transform your life from mediocre to miraculous, then just say the word, because that's exactly how the magic begins: by a simple and sincere thank you.

Seldom do we really stop and think about the power of giving thanks. When it comes to being grateful, what we give out, we are going to get back. Whether it be to our Creator, a family member, a friend, a stranger or a pet, it will return to us many times multiplied. I believe the degree that we choose to incorporate gratitude into our daily lives is going to directly influence our level of abundance and joy.

Considering all the options we have to improve our lives, there are very few things that will serve us better than understanding the power of being appreciative. Although we all equally possess the ability to be thankful, the extent to which we choose to express our appreciation varies immensely. If everyone were more aware of how intimately gratitude and happiness are bound, our collective level of joy would increase exponentially.

Undeniably, a happy life will be a rich life, and although I am not necessarily speaking in terms of monetary value, I am also not excluding it either. Having read *The Science of Getting Rich*, by Wallace Wattles I am convinced that he understood this concept exceedingly well when he wrote, " Many people who order their lives rightly in all other ways are kept in poverty by their lack of gratitude."

I imagine that we all like to think of ourselves as grateful, but, are we really, and to what extent?

For starters, we might profess that we never fail to say thank you for a gift or service provided. That's good. We certainly aim to say grace before dinner..... well, at least before our Thanksgiving meal for sure. Getting better. Finally, who hasn't gratefully announced, "thank God it's Friday!" Definitely a decent start, but gratitude is so much more. We tend to take many things for granted, yet when we really stop and think about all the ways in which we are blessed, gratitude takes on a whole new meaning.

Gratitude is effortless. However, because the scope and magnitude of being grateful is so all encompassing, we might find ourselves wondering where and how to even begin.

So, where do we start? Well, how about the moment we wake? Starting the morning off by being thankful is a perfect way to lay the groundwork for a much happier, and more successful day. If our first thoughts are expressions of gratitude, we are essentially rolling out the red carpet toward an exciting day full of unlimited potential.

If we don't take that moment of thankfulness at the beginning of the day, we can get so caught up in our busy and hurried lives that we will just hit the ground running, never stopping until the end of the day when exhaustion finally overwhelms us. At this point we stumble back into bed too tired to do anything but worry about all of the stuff we didn't get done. Come dawn, we begin anew, right where we left off. We continue on with this circular pattern until the wheels fall off and we are forced to stop and reevaluate our priorities.

Should we veer off track or end up heading in the wrong direction, the Universe will always find a way to slow us down and help us reset our course. We may not always realize it, but the Divine is constantly looking out for us so that we may make the best of our lives. Still, it is our responsibility to take notice, and to be grateful for what it is trying so hard to help us with.

For instance, a common cold frequently has a way of showing up precisely when it's the last thing we have time for. We might think that we are being unfairly punished by a less than benevolent Creator, but more likely, there is a very good reason why it manifests when we already have far too much going on in our lives. Getting sick just might be how the Universe reminds us to take some time to care for ourselves. When we allow ourselves some quiet isolation and much needed rest, notice how we immediately begin to feel better. Looking at the situation from this perspective, our feelings of irritation might hastily be replaced with gratitude. Conversely, when all of our attention is focused on the fact that we are missing something, or that something is wrong, our thinking is counterproductive to what we wish to accomplish: restoring what we have lost. It doesn't make any difference what we believe we are missing, be it our good health or our wealth, at this point, gratitude is often the last thing we are considering. However, it is exactly what is required to turn the situation around. We have to start feeling better mentally to attract a positive outcome in the physical realm, and what better way than by giving thanks.

A useful exercise when we are in need of an emotional boost is to focus on what we are grateful for. Whether we focus on one specific thing, or mentally list everything that we are appreciative of, this exercise will always be enjoyable and yield great results.

When we are feeling brighter emotionally, and are, as a result, healthier mentally and physically, we can be certain that we are again heading in the right direction. Because it is virtually impossible to feel both grateful and despondent at the exact same moment, we will always feel better and happier whenever we are feeling genuine gratitude.

Of course the happier we are, the more grateful we become. Now here is a cyclic pattern that we definitely want to continue.

Perhaps now it will be a little easier to recognize that there may actually be some intrinsic value in our apparent setbacks. Our newfound clarity of vision has allowed us to discover the blessing in the proverbial darkness. Now we can appreciate the wonder in a multitude of things that we had previously taken for granted.

Take water for instance. The elixir of life. We cannot live without it, but how many times in a day do we remember to be thankful for it? When our hearts are full of gratitude the answer will be most likely be, "quite often."

Interestingly enough, when I set out to write this chapter, I happened to come across *The Hidden Messages in Water*, by Masaru Emoto. Although I had heard of his work, for some unknown reason I had not taken the time to search for his beautiful little book. Of course, as the old proverb states, "When the student is ready the teacher will appear." All of a sudden, there it was, just waiting to be discovered. Isn't it wonderful how the Universe works!

By photographing water crystals, Emoto was able to capture how water molecules respond to our thoughts, our words, and our feelings. The most magnificent crystals were formed when pure spring water was exposed to expressions of love and gratitude. Since our bodies are approximately 70% water, is it any wonder that we respond so well to gratitude?

I might compare my everyday happiness to the fizzle and pop rising up in an effervescent drink, but whenever I experience an overwhelming sense of gratitude, I cannot help but to feel a fountain of pure joy bubbling up within me. It is at these times that I experience the parallel of how I am feeling with the image of crystal clear waters overflowing from an artesian well. Incredibly, we were blessed with this very luxury on the century farm where I grew up. Our well was a perpetual source of pure and cool refreshment, the overflow spilling onto, and running along a hollowed out cedar log covered in a soft, green moss. Now even to me this sounds like an embellishment, but that is exactly what it was like. Regardless of the season, there at the bottom of a steep and rocky hill, in the middle of the cow pasture, we had a continuously running fountain.

Of course, luxury comes with a price. The cost to have this precious water pumped to the house required the digging of a six foot deep trench, hundreds of feet uphill, just to lay the piping for the project. Honestly, how my father managed to slave away at the foundry all day, keep up with the never ending farm chores, and complete this trench, is beyond comprehension. He managed however, so that we could all reap the benefits of his efforts.

Unfortunately, I don't recall thanking him for that massive undertaking, for as children there are many things we simply take for granted and cannot truly appreciate. As adults, we really should be more aware of the abundance that surrounds us, but despite being a little older and maybe a bit wiser, we sometimes still fail to see it, and thus, forget to give thanks. Too often we are missing the miraculous in the seemingly ordinary.

If we should offer a cup of cold and refreshing water to someone who is thirsty and they respond with a heartfelt thank you, we would both feel uplifted and grateful; they for having received the gift and we for having offered it. We can transform any act of kindness into a blessing by our gratitude. No matter how great or small the gesture, when we remember to say thank you, the energy in and all around us expands and is elevated. Indeed, there is enormous rejuvenating power in the simple act of offering thanks.

## Living Well

Our memories, like water, are restorative and precious. Without memory, we lose our way. Without water we thirst, and eventually perish. We must remember that there is a pipeline that connects us to our Creator, and to each other. Through this line flows our gratitude, and in return we receive an abundance of joy, for they are essentially one and the same.

When all that was once ordinary, becomes extraordinary, and our world is filled with anticipation, excitement, and joy, we can be certain that we have embraced gratitude. All of a sudden, regardless of our situation, we can now greet the day with a genuine smile, and a deep and profound, "thank you!"

Since we all wish to live a life of abundance, we will do well to remember that when we are truly grateful for the small blessings in our lives, we are planting tiny seeds of happiness that cannot help but mature into an abundance of joy, and a joyful life is an abundant life.

## Chapter 8

# Knocking on Heavens Door

*"Ask and you will receive;
seek, and you will find; knock and the door
will be opened for you."*

MATTHEW 7:7

Another wonderful season is coming to a close. Officially it may still be summer, but reminders are everywhere that soon it will not be. The days are getting shorter, the nights cooler. The incessant chirping of crickets either lulling us to sleep, or keeping us very much awake. Then again, perhaps the reason sleep is eluding us isn't so much the crickets singing, but rather all the noise that is nowhere other than in our own little heads.

A cacophony of endless conversations going every which way but ours. Our cup is indeed overflowing, but not exactly with joy.

Trying times. We have all experienced them. To be sure, there will be points in our life when we will feel that more is being asked of us than we are humanly capable of managing. Some days we will not know how to solve a particular problem. At times, we will not know how or when to let go of one. Night after night we might lie awake trying to figure out how to get rid of all our troubles. Unfortunately, the only thing that we manage to lose is sleep.

When times are especially trying, we might suddenly be inclined to start praying, even if we never have before. If we did pray before, chances are we will pray more intensely. However, when there are no visible signs that our requests or our prayers are being answered, or even heard for that matter, we start to wonder if anyone is even listening. We might be thinking, "Hello! Is anyone home? I've been searching, I'm asking, and I'm knocking, but nobody seems to be answering." So what can we do with a cup full of suffering? Short answer; drop everything into God's lap. With the words "Thy will be done," we can let it go.

A number of years ago my mother-in-law came to visit bringing with her a couple of rubber squeaky toys for our two small dogs, Buddy and Sophie. These unusual rubber monsters were about the size of an orange and looked to be a cross between a sea urchin and Bigfoot. Sophie was not impressed with her new toy, nor the company. Buddy, on the other hand, immediately became completely obsessed with his gift. Despite its strange appearance, its squeak resembled that of a newborn baby, and somehow Buddy determined that it was indeed just that. With the utmost care he carried this baby monster with him everywhere for three days. Ever so gently, careful to not make it cry, he would lay it down in front of himself for only as long as it took him to eat or do his business. Then off to his blanket they would go where, setting it by his chest, he would give it occasional reassuring kisses. When Sophie had first joined our family, he had cared for her in much the same way. Now she was being completely ignored, displaced by an impostor.

I could see that she was missing her big brother's attention, and it was clear that Buddy was getting weary of his self assigned parenting role. However, when I tried taking the toy away, he just sat at the closet where it was hidden and whined. It was a difficult time for all of us. Then on the third night with what must have been his last remaining bit of energy,

Buddy jumped up onto the bed, took a few exhausted steps towards me, and unceremoniously dropped his pseudo baby in my lap. With big, brown, imploring eyes he looked up, and just as clearly as if he had spoken the words, I knew that he was telling me, "I'm done! You look after this for me, I cannot do it any more." Without waiting for a reply he turned, made his way to the end of the bed, and collapsed in a heap of white fluff. After giving one big sigh of relief, he immediately fell asleep, as only dogs can do.

When it all seems like too much, we, like Buddy, must have complete faith and be willing to drop everything into our master's lap. Trusting that God will take perfect care of our burden, crickets or no crickets, we can then easily drift off into a peaceful sleep.

Anyone can assume the role of selfless nurturer and caregiver. I believe however, that mothers are renowned for taking on this task with unequaled passion. There is a bond between mother and child that reaches far beyond what words can adequately define. Considering the depths of this demanding and lifelong position, I am inclined to think that collectively speaking, more prayers will probably be spoken by mothers than the rest of the world combined. Anomalies aside, mothers simply want what is best for their children. Isn't that exactly what our Creator wants for us? Maybe it's common sense, maybe it's a sixth sense, but mother or not, I believe it just makes sense to seek guidance and support through prayer.

Some may claim that prayer is for the weak and the naive. I disagree. I believe that prayer, like gratitude, connects us to each other, and to a power which is infinitely greater than ourselves. "Seek and ye shall find." If we wish to experience life to the fullest we must continuously search for knowledge and strength, both within as well as outside of ourselves. We needn't blindly accept what others might try to force upon us. Instead, we need to be more discerning. By searching our hearts and by listening to the Spirit within, we can then choose the spiritual path that will be best for us.

We can be sure we are on the correct path when what we find uplifts us, and all those around us. We know we are on the right path when what we find aims not to oppress and separate, but rather empowers and bring us closer together. We know we are on the right path when what we find promotes both peace and passion, allowing us to believe in and also create miracles. It may very well happen through traditional means, but if not, supporting the unconventional are the words spoken by Jesus, "He who is not against us, is for us."

When the disciples asked Jesus how to pray, Jesus taught them the Lord's Prayer. Searching for peace, we will often find repose in the Serenity prayer. And yet, in the words of Meister Eckhart "If the only prayer you ever say in your entire life is thank you, it will be enough."

Prayer, without question, is immensely personal. Everyone will express and experience it in unique ways. Much like with colour, we may all have our preferences and favorites, but it does not mean that any of the other hues are any less beautiful. Still, if either prayer or beautiful colours are to enhance our life, we have to choose those which will be most comfortable and meaningful for us.

Sometimes we will petition the saints, and sometimes departed family. We might ask our guardian angels to intervene, or consult our spirit guides for direction. God, Yahveh, Jesus, Krishna, Buddha, Allah, Jehovah, The Great Spirit.....enter all other faiths and spiritual beliefs, and we can be certain that there is no shortage of available help in the Divine assistance department. Nevertheless, we have to remember to ask so that we might receive. It sounds simple enough and yet we know it isn't always so easy or straightforward, otherwise, we would have all won the lottery by now. I have no magic formula for instantaneously manifesting monetary wealth, but, if we truly want to feel richer quickly, our thoughts and prayers must come from a place of gratitude and love, rather than from scarcity and fear.

"Ask and you will receive," call it blind faith, eternal optimism, or the Law of Attraction. Regardless of the name we choose, the key to success is, of course, remembering to focus on what we want, not on what we fear or dislike. Whether we are asking or praying, although in my opinion it is essentially the same thing, it is important to consider the words we are using. Do they truly reflect what we desire? If the word "don't" is included, you might want to rephrase your request.

Consider for a moment how the following statement makes you feel. "Please don't let me make a big mistake and fail." Not exactly reassuring or uplifting. It is a request that is filled with fearful thoughts, and focuses only on what we do not want. This approach offers us absolutely no comfort or confidence.

With gratitude and a positive focus we can transform any appeal into a potential miracle. Notice the dramatic contrast in the same, but very differently worded prayer: "Thank you for helping me to be careful and accurate, so that I may succeed in all that I do." Now this is how we can instantly feel more peaceful, trusting, and joyful. This is the alchemy of applying gratitude to all our thoughts and prayers, and this is how we turn straw into gold.

Remember, no one religion, faith, or group holds the monopoly on prayer; it can be as individual and unique as we are diverse.

Life without prayer. What would it be like to omit something so crucial to our well-being and happiness? It wouldn't necessarily be anything we could see, but I suspect that there would be a definite void at the center of our being. We might try filling this space with any number of things, but I wonder if regardless of our efforts we would always have the feeling that something was missing; a day without sunshine, a night without dreams.

Until we are called forth, we are not likely to see all that is behind heaven's door. Still, whenever we knock, either to share our joy, or to pour out our sorrows, we hope and trust that someone will be there to welcome us unconditionally.

I cannot fathom a life without prayer. For every extraordinary day, and each exquisite night, to whom would we offer our thanks? In times of darkness, suffering, or fear, to whom would we cry out? And if on occasion life should happen to fill our cup with more than we can possibly bear, into who's lap could we drop all our burdens?

## Chapter 9
# The Price of Magic

"If you knew Who walks beside you
on the way that you have chosen,
fear would be impossible."

A COURSE IN MIRACLES

My mother was an extraordinary woman. She was remarkably strong both mentally and physically, and there were very few things she was afraid of. At the age of nineteen, she endured the invasion of Poland at the start of World War II. She worked for two years as a lumberjack in a Russian work camp, after being deported to Siberia. Following her release, she travelled to Uganda where she spent six long years in a refugee camp. There she chased a gorilla through the African jungle, didn't catch it, but did catch malaria twice. When the war ended, she immigrated to Canada; a country she knew nothing about except that it was the place where she was to marry a man whom she had not seen in six war torn years. And what frightened her? A little group of trick or treaters!

It was the last day of October, and my father had left for work. Regrettably he had forgotten to tell his wife about a particular celebration of ours called Halloween. It was a tradition which she had never experienced, nor even heard of for that matter. Oops! In addition, although she could communicate in several different languages, English was not yet one of them. Not good.

When darkness fell and a gathering of unusually dressed children arrived on her doorstep, she could not fathom why they were there, nor understand what they were asking of her. So, she gave them each a quarter, (quite a substantial amount in 1949) then hid in the dark for the rest of the evening, anxiously awaiting my father's return.

The fact is, everyone is afraid of something. That this is the only time I can recall her speaking of being fearful is astounding. I wish I could say that I inherited her courage, but I did not. On my refrigerator I have a small collection of magnets, five separate words that you can arrange any which way you like. They were a welcomed gift that happened to come in the mail one day. Creating a much needed affirmation, I have arranged them to read, I am strong, growing courageous! I know that this is possible. I just have to remember and believe. After all, I am my mother's daughter!

Growing courageous. It is a process. A process that involves recognizing fear for the illusion that it is, and then learning to let go of it.

Although magic tricks appear very real, we all know that they are only an illusion. The same can be said of fear. Because it is so convincing, it can trick us into believing all sorts of things that are simply not true. Often times the most frightening illusions are those of our own making. When we believe in, and cling to our fears, the potential for all kinds of joy and adventure will disappear from our life just like a magician's vanishing act. Nothing will diminish our world more certainly than fear.

Now remember, just like magic, we can get it all back. The loss is only an illusion. Everything is right there in front of us, we just can't see it, or grasp it. Our blindfold and shackles are our fears. So the real trick will be learning to escape from our self induced restraints. If we can succeed in removing the blindfold, then we will be able to see clearly enough to grasp the precious key that will unlock the remaining chains that bind us. It's a process!

We have to remember that since we are never completely alone, sometimes it just makes sense to ask for help. Something I should have learned a long time ago.

Staying home alone was definitely something my younger brother Wally and I dreaded. Convinced that our century farmhouse was haunted by an angry ghost that would come and go at random, we were on constant high alert. I must admit, we were more than a little skittish. Although this entity seemed to have an affinity for one particular upstairs room and would often make it clear to us that he did not appreciate our presence there, we could never be sure whether the rest of the house was off limits as well.

Needless to say, we grew up intimidated and afraid of what we could not see, but could definitely feel. Be it day, evening, or night, if we had any other option besides staying home alone, we would take it. As a result of this fear we found ourselves spending one unforgettable and incredibly long summer day in the city.

## The Price of Magic

Whether we declined to go or were not invited, I can't be sure, but our parents had planned a trip to the Niagara belt to visit friends and pick fresh fruit, and this full day affair did not include us.

Rather than leave a six and ten year old alone on an isolated farm for so many hours, our mother decided that my little brother and I would spend the day in town with my dad's best friend, Mike. At the time we thought it fortuitous that although his wife was to tag along with my parents, he had chosen to forfeit the trip.

Unbeknownst to us, we were about to escape being isolated and alone in the country, with an ominous presence which we could not see but were sure was there, only to be alone and isolated in the city with a man that we were sure was there but we could not see. Neither did we expect to endure the longest and most pointless fast of our lives.

Early in the morning on that fateful day, we were hastily dropped off with absolutely nothing other than the clothes we were wearing. Left to do as we chose, we immediately headed out to the park, which was conveniently located just outside of Mike's backyard. We played there until our hungry little stomachs indicated it was time for lunch, and persuaded us to return to the house.

After helping ourselves to water from the bathroom tap, we quietly sat down in the living room, anticipating that soon we might be fed. We waited there until long after the distinctive din of flatware upon china could no longer be heard. No offering of any sort was forthcoming. I remember seriously debating whether we should ask for a piece of bread, or something to drink, but either we were too polite, or too afraid, and we never followed through with any sort of request. Eventually we grew both discouraged and restless, so again we headed outdoors.

For a moment, our spirits lifted. We had to pass through the vegetable garden to access the park! With a little luck, perhaps we might find something edible to stave off even a tiny bit of our hunger. As luck would have it, all we found were empty vines. Feeling somewhat desperate, we considered unearthing and sharing a raw potato, but then fearing the repercussions of eating it uncooked, I determined it best we abandon the plan, dashing Wally's hopes in the process.

Refusing defeat, our next strategy was to look for loose change in the park. Perhaps good fortune would rain down and offer us someone's lost nickel or dime. Bearing our newly found treasure, we could then head to the corner store and purchase a popsicle or ice cream cone. With dogged determination we combed through a sizable portion of the park's sunbaked grass, without success. Our tenacity knew no bounds, so we extended our search. Unfortunately, after thoroughly scrutinizing the ground all the way to the variety store, we found nothing but debris. All our efforts were in vain.

Completely disheartened, we conceded to wait. Time stood still. I honestly cannot tell you what we did in the remaining hours, apart from listening to each others' stomachs growl. I do know that we would have to wait for our shadows to grow long and distorted before salvation finally arrived in the form of a pale blue Chevy sedan. Never would we be happier to see our parents' car.

The last clear image I have of that fateful day is that of Wally diving headlong into the back seat, and immediately cramming into his face the first piece of precious fruit he could lay his hands on. If you can picture a Charles Dickens scene where a starving street urchin might find his first edible morsel of the week, then you have a perfect visual. My mother was surprised. Perhaps even a little alarmed. Before she could inquire, like a drunkard shouting his uncensored thoughts, Wally bellowed, " He never fed us all daaay!" Although somewhat aghast by his lack of restraint, I remained silent, for I was far more disappointed in myself. Because of my fears I had failed him.

Capitalizing on the entertainment value, Wally and I have repeated this story many times over. If we focus on the humorous aspects, it can be quite amusing. But, if you're wondering what it has to do with fear and the Law of Attraction, I can assure you, just about everything.

We knew that Mike would do anything for our dad. We understood that Mike cared about us too, so it didn't make any sense that he would purposely try to starve us. He later claimed to his very annoyed wife, that having none of his own, he simply didn't know what kids ate. Now you have to admit, that's pretty funny! As ridiculous as that might sound, should it be the truth, all he had to do was ask. Unfortunately, much like my mother once was afraid of those children on Halloween, Mike too, was afraid of a couple of little kids. Other than being painfully thin, I really don't think we were that scary.

It makes perfect sense to me now that that particular summer day so long ago could not have played out any differently. Our fears of being all alone, kept us alone. Different place, similar situation. Furthermore, how on earth could we have expected to receive any kind of food, when all we could think about was the fact that we were not being fed? Remember the laws of attraction are always in action. What a different day we would have had if only we had thought about what we really wanted, and then simply asked for it. Undoubtedly, we would have received.

We leave behind some of our childhood fears, while others will follow us as surely as our shadow. I left that angry ghost back at the old farmhouse long ago, but unfortunately I took the rest of my fears with me. For decades, every day that I set off to work I shouldered this needless burden of imagined fears, like a heavy sack of potatoes.

Fear can be a very persistent and ominous presence, eventually taking on a life of its own. Left unchecked, it can and will create total havoc in our lives. Trust me, I speak from many years of experience. Because I lived in constant fear that something scary might happen, it usually did. Consequently most of my shifts as a nurse were either exhausting or downright frightening. Without understanding why, I felt helpless to make any effective changes.

Although I have thoroughly enjoyed a variety of books on the Law of Attraction, including the wonderful series by Esther and Jerry Hicks, it was not until I read *The Secret*, by Rhonda Byrne, that I finally understood and could truly appreciate the immense power that our thoughts have over our lives.

Trying to piece together a puzzle without the original box is a daunting task. Still, we can all appreciate the excitement that follows when that one little piece fits in perfectly and suddenly the entire picture comes to life. I knew with absolute certainty that I could neither wish nor pray my fears away. I never would have guessed that it would take me more than thirty years to discover the secret. The secret that would allow me to control the monster that was, in fact, controlling me.

Thus it was an epiphany to realize that by focusing on this unwanted monster of fear, I was keeping it so well fed that it just kept growing larger. In order for my fears to diminish, all I really had to do was turn my attention to, and center my intention on the peace and calm that I longed for. I didn't have to slay the dragon. I simply had to tame it. Mark Twain must have known this a long time ago when he wrote, "Courage is resistance to fear, mastery of fear-not absence of fear."

Without the constant looming presence of fear casting its darkened shadow, my days became considerably brighter and my life suddenly felt a lot more magical. I now choose my thoughts wisely, careful to ensure that fear is not continuously among them.

In the classic fairy tale story of Rumpelstiltskin, the strange little man with the long nose always asks the miller's daughter for something in return before he agrees to spin the straw into gold for her. First she offers him her necklace, the second time her ring, but having nothing of value the third and final time, she promises to give up her first born. She agrees to this out of fear. If the straw isn't turned into gold for the king, she and her father will be punished.

You might think that this is just a silly old fairy tale, but the truth is, the most foolish and outrageous things are often done out of fear.

This fairy tale also gives us the impression that magic can only happen if we first offer something in exchange. Perhaps this is true. However, I am quite certain it is not your first born. It is simply your fears. Unfortunately, we tend to cling to our fears as tightly as we do to our children. At some point we must learn to let go.

If our hands are tightly grasping fear, how can we ever hope to welcome into our lives the abundance that awaits us? Just as we need to ask in order to receive, we need to have open minds and open hands so that we might appreciate, and be prepared to accept the gift being offered. When we learn to give up our fears, we free ourselves and allow all kinds of *real* magic into our lives.

Never underestimate the power within you. Remember, you are the master magician. You can release your fears so that you may take hold of your life and embrace what your heart feels with the most passion. You just have to believe that it is possible and know that you are never completely alone.

I wish I could profess to you that I am now fearless, but that claim would simply not be true. I am not discouraged however, for I can honestly say that since discovering the teachings of the Law of Attraction a whole new world has opened up for me. In this space I am happier and far more courageous than I could have ever imagined. This is a world where I am constantly learning how to create real magic, and it is here that everyday miracles are readily experienced and recognized.

# Chapter 10
# A Whole New World

> "There are only two ways to live your life. One is as though nothing is a miracle, the other is as if everything is."
>
> ALBERT EINSTEIN

*W*ho among the faithful doesn't love a good angel story? I like to think that we all do. Perhaps I am being presumptuous? Maybe even a little naive? Nevertheless, I believe that sharing our stories about the miraculous elevates the spirit of both the story teller and the person with whom the story is shared.

Our most passionate recollections of Divine assistance will often depict dramatic rescues or inexplicable aid at a crucial time. Far more subtle but just as poignant, we might recount a time when a peaceful and reassuring presence carried us through a particularly challenging or difficult period. Regardless, the common thread is that we believe the extent, quality or direction of our life was largely influenced by something or someone not of this world, that is, our angels.

Sometimes we are immediately aware of the miracle that has taken place, other times, it is years before we realize the magnificence of a particular incident. For me one such event, although vivid in my memory, is also destined to remain cloaked in mystery. This story dates back several decades, so for those of you who never experienced winter in rural Canada in the nineteen sixties, I assure you it was a time very different from our present day reality. It was a time when freezing one's butt off wasn't just an expression. Indoor plumbing that included a flushing toilet, for many, was still just a wish on their very short Christmas list. Our friends were not as fortunate as we were. They most likely did not have a father willing to work twenty hours a day, and one who was able to do whatever he set his mind to. Thankfully, with six kids and four adults living under one roof, our dad believed that the outhouse would be more useful as backup, rather than as a main bathroom. So we were blessed with a working indoor toilet, and hot and cold running water. Yeah!

We also had the luxury of a deep claw-foot bathtub, most likely salvaged from an old farmhouse and bought at an auction. It wasn't in the best condition, but it beat bathing in an oversized tin wash basin set in the middle of the kitchen floor. This much nicer setup allowed us all to have at least some semblance of privacy for Saturday night baths.

Although a distant reality, plumbing to the barn would not be completed until time allowed for another ditch digging marathon. Prior to that time, the water source for the cattle was the pond at the bottom of a steep hill. Every morning and evening the cows had to make the long trek to the reservoir and then circle back to the barn. To ensure they had access to the water, a hole had to be chopped in the ice twice a day during the winter months.

This task was just one of the many things on my mother's long list of regular chores. Factoring in the considerable distance from the house, it was a time consuming process. So one particularly mild winter afternoon she sent me off to check whether the hole had frozen over. She hoped that I would return with the favorable news that the ice didn't need to be chopped again that day. It never occurred to either one of us that the far better news would be......that I return.

In spite of the mild temperature it was still mid winter, so dressed from head to toe in heavy wool, I left the house weighing considerably more than I had a moment earlier, and headed off down the hill.

When I arrived at the pond, I was instantly dismayed to find that a very thin film of ice had formed over the hole. I wondered whether the cows would realize that the ice was extremely fragile. Would they know enough to tap it with their nose so that it would break apart, or would the thin barrier deter them from even trying? No surprise that I was uncertain, I had only just turned five.

I did not want the cows to walk away thirsty, nor did I want to disappoint my mother, so the most reasonable solution to both problems was to give the ice a light tap, with my little foot. Well, in an instant I definitely solved one of problems. I crashed through the barely frozen surface, and slipped deep into the frigid water. I was then faced with a new problem.....how to get out?

By holding onto the thick ice at the edge of the hole, and by standing on the tip of my toes, I was able to keep my head above the water. I could feel the sloped floor of the pond with my right foot, but my left floated freely in deeper waters. The weight of my wool clothing, now saturated, had multiplied many times over. It was impossible for me to hoist myself out.

I can't recall being cold or frightened, but I do remember thinking that I must figure a way out of this mess, because no one was going to be strolling by anytime soon to help me. With that thought in mind, I immediately saw a clear vision of the pond in summer. The cows invariably would leave numerous hoof prints near the water's edge. Although the holes were deep, the displaced mud also created significantly elevated ridges. I was certain that if I simply got turned around, and felt for the highest point with my foot, I would have enough height to extricate myself from this potentially lethal trap.

Indeed the plan was successful, but I was soaking wet from head to toe and I was afraid that if I returned home as such, my mother would be angry. So I decided to walk home very slowly, in hopes that by the time I arrived, my clothes would be dry. If you've ever been stopped behind a school bus that is dropping off a group of youngsters between the age of four and six, hopefully you're not in a hurry. You can see that they are moving, but is it really forward?

After a couple of hundred meters at a ridiculously slow pace, I finally reached the yard. Upon seeing the clothes line, I suddenly remembered that wet clothes don't dry in the winter, they freeze solid. Yikes! This realization immediately prompted me to move faster. Thinking back, I have to question, how it was possible for me to remain outside for that length of time, sopping wet, and never register the feeling of being cold?

Just as my mother stepped out onto the porch, wondering what was causing my delay, I entered the yard. I don't imagine I could have possibly understood the emotion, but by the look on her face, I instantly knew I was not in trouble. Moments later, I was again up to my neck in water. This time, in an old claw foot bath tub. This time, I was warm and safe, with my mother watching over me.

Maybe I was still at the wonderful age when interacting with angels is perfectly normal, because at the time, I don't recall thinking that anything out of the ordinary had occurred that day. Considering what could have been, I imagine my mother felt differently.

## A Whole New World

Although there have been many instances in my life where I believe angels intervened, I chose this particular story. Not because it is extraordinary, but rather, because it is not. Other than being alive, I have no proof that angels helped me that day. I saw no glowing apparition. No wings. No voices. I do believe however, that it was Divine intervention that saved me.

Sometimes when we hear stories that are outrageously astonishing, we either don't believe them, or we wonder why nothing equally spectacular ever happens to us. Perhaps we are failing to see the miracle in the ordinary. Often, we attribute our everyday "coincidences" to chance. Maybe there is more to our "good luck" story than initially meets the eye. Could it be that we are being assisted far more frequently than we realize?

I am not an expert on angels. Still, I believe that angels are God's Divine messengers and our protectors, and that they are always by our side. Considering that there are a number of occasions in life where we could use a helping hand, we should remember to call upon the angels often, so that we may benefit from the peace and strength that they provide.

Doreen Virtue, American author and founder of Angel Therapy, teaches us that whenever we see the sequential numbers 444 we are being reminded that loving and supporting angels are all around us. I see that particular sequence of numbers often. My spirit never fails to be uplifted. What a wonderful reminder for us to pause just long enough to say, thank you to our angels.

Whether we believe in angels or whether we do not, it doesn't change the fact that angels will be an ever present part of our life. Unfortunately, it isn't easy to convince the unbeliever, as angels are a lot like miracles, very difficult, if not impossible, to prove. Yet, to the one experiencing them, they are undeniable.

When we remember that we are never completely alone, we can approach things that we once found intimidating with a new found sense of confidence. When we call for and receive a little help from our friends, human or otherwise, life really does get a lot easier. Just like true friends, angels ask for nothing in return.

When I set out to write this chapter I couldn't seem to get past the first paragraph. For weeks, absolutely nothing! Despite being slightly perplexed, I was not worried. Then one day at work, I happened to mention that the chapter I was working on would be devoted to angels. The genuine interest and

## A Whole New World

excitement that followed was most encouraging. It was the inspiration that I needed. The following morning I sat down to write, and words suddenly began to flow effortlessly and freely.

Upon finishing the last sentence for the day, I glanced over at my automatic word counter; 9,444 words. What a thoughtful and brilliant way for the angels to confirm their presence. The significance of the numbers was not lost on me. I smiled and said, "thank you."

Life really is full of miracles, unfortunately often times we just don't recognize them as such. When our awareness expands and we realize that we are part of something bigger than ourselves, it is amazing how suddenly what was once ordinary, becomes extraordinary.

## Chapter 11
# The Heart of Happiness

> "When one door of happiness closes,
> another opens; but often we look so
> long at the closed door that we do
> not see the one which has been opened for us."
> HELLEN KELLER

Coming across the right book at precisely the right time is a blessing that I have encountered often in my life. Regardless of the number of times that this has occurred over the years, it never fails to surprise and delight me. Still, when I think about the mysterious way in which a little gem called *Happy for No Reason,* by Marci Shimoff came into my awareness, I cannot help but feel an enhanced sense of joy and gratitude. Filled with uplifting stories, and fascinating happiness studies, this book is sure to elevate anyone's spirit. Despite considering myself a very happy person, my level of joy noticeably increased with each turn of the page.

It was just an ordinary day at the local library, searching for inspiration. As usual, I was confident that the ideal book would present itself, brimming with what I needed to discover and learn the most. I have an ongoing trust and appreciation for the angelic guidance which, upon request, will always be forthcoming. I never fail to ask. With a little Divine assistance, in record time, I made what I thought were two great choices. After scanning the books through the self checkout, I was soon heading out the door. Suddenly, I looked down and was completely mystified to discover *Happy for No Reason* on top of my bundle. Huh! How on earth had that happened? I had in fact chosen two books, but this was definitely not one of them. However, judging by the title it appeared to me that this could potentially be a very interesting read and although I am usually quite happy, I figured that there is always room for improvement. I decided to keep the stowaway, and thanked the unseen angels for intervening.

Considering the unusual way that I came across this particular book, you have to admit that it is rather incredible how the Universe can string together any number of ordinary events and create an extraordinary outcome. Of course we have to be willing to do our part. Since I hadn't consciously chosen it, I just as easily could have put the book back. I didn't though, as I believed that within the pages of this text was something important that the Universe wanted me to discover. Indeed, I was not mistaken. The ripple effect that this little miracle has had on my life has been enormous. Clearly the Universe is out to help us live a life filled with joy.

    I honestly believe that our natural state is one of happiness. When we are happy, we are in harmony with our true essence, everything feels just right. In contrast, when we are living without joy in our lives, all will feel out of sync and foreign; our authentic self knowing that something crucial is missing. In light of this reality, many will spend their entire life in pursuit of happiness. Unfortunately, searching in all the wrong places yields disappointing results and will only leave us wondering why happiness is so elusive. Similarly, convinced that happiness is "out there," we often fool ourselves into believing that we will be happy *when* we finally have whatever it is we are wishing for.

## Pebbles of Joy

What we fail to realize is that joy works the other way around. Joy comes from within. When we discover and understand the essence of true joy, we stir the embers so that the glow within us begins to burn brighter. When our light shines outward it also reflects joy back to us. Everything in our life begins to fall into better alignment with our wishes.

Perhaps this is in part what Nichiren Daishonin meant when he wrote, "If one lights a fire for others one will brighten one's own way." If we are all part of the same Universal energy, it makes sense that what we do for another, we do for ourselves. No wonder the smallest act of kindness can yield such positive results. In my experience some of the happiest and most peaceful people have a profound understanding of this Universal connection. With a mission to make the world a better place, these individuals passionately aspire to bring this awareness to others. Our job is to believe!

Of course, that is easy enough for those of us born with an abundance of happy hormones, but I imagine that there will be times when believing in anything might seem inconceivable if one is struggling with depression.

## The Heart of Happiness

Still, I believe there is always hope and that one should never stop searching for a solution. Keeping an open mind can prompt one to at least be curious, if not immediately happy. As long as we are willing to ask questions, the mind must respond with answers. If the answer isn't helpful or positive, maybe we need to ask a different question, or possibly a different person. Perhaps the ultimate question we need to ask ourselves is this: "Is the story we are telling ourselves even true?" Maybe it is. Maybe it isn't. Whatever the truth may be, we can always change the remainder of our story. Remember, it all begins with one tiny thought. You owe it to yourself to make it a good one. Just one, single, grateful thought can be the beginning of your new and better story. Your new and happier life.

We all have access to happiness. It is not "out there" somewhere but rather, shining right here within our hearts. We must take the time to be still, to silence the noise both inside and outside of our minds. In a peaceful lull, our spirits can connect to the magnificence of Universal energy and know pure love, peace, joy, and perfect contentment. We may not be adept at frequenting this extraordinary state of being, but there is enormous power in the awareness of it. The more we seek out this connection, the happier we will be. If at our center we are at peace, we can still feel joy regardless of what is occurring in our lives.

Never forget that our true essence is one of joy, peace and loving kindness. Together may we find our true joy.

## Chapter 12
# The Best Present

> "Gain happiness by living in the present, without regret for the past or fear of the future."
> JONATHAN LOCKWOOD HUIE

*I*n the softness of the morning light when all is still and quiet we can find a little piece of heaven. The joy of silence and solitude will soon give way to stirrings of life and laughter. Time stands still for only as long as we are willing to comply. There is no going back, only moving forward; eventually returning from whence we came. Enjoy each moment. Make all of them count!

We search for that place where everything is in order. A place that is still, no chaos, no uncertainty. Yet, it is the element of surprise, the anticipation, that excites us, that drives us forward. We long for change and then resist it. How do we find the balance? How do we embrace peace, relax, and let go? How do we know that every moment is just as it should be? How do we stay true to ourselves and to others, live by what we know to be right? Just as the answers can be found in being still, the answer is of course, by being still.

As I begin this chapter, the Christmas season is upon us. Talk about impeccable timing. This wonderful gift called synchronicity is just another delightful reminder that we are never in this alone. The choreography of the Universe is timed to perfection. Pause and take notice!

Although every family that celebrates Christmas will have its own unique customs and traditions, most will incorporate some version of a Christmas tree. Fresh and fragrant, artificial, ceramic, or merely a lowly branch, whatever it may be, we take time out of our busy schedule, and adorn it with light and love.

We may not have the means to place gifts below the boughs, but I believe that on some intrinsic level we all sense that the tree is a wonderful gift in and of itself. Beautifully and eloquently, it reminds us of the true meaning of Christmas.

## The Best Present

Inspiring peace, hope, love and joy, it bestows upon us the very same gifts Jesus blessed us with by his birth on that very first Christmas Day.

Many of us have found peaceful sanctuary just by sitting quietly in a darkened room illuminated only by the soft glow from our Yuletide evergreen. No matter how sparse the branches or meager the trimmings, we can feel the love emanating from all that it embodies, every cherished ornament reflecting back to us joyful memories of Christmases gone by. Within each brightly coloured ball, we see cheerful visions of Christmases yet to come. Mesmerized, the line between past and present blurs. Twinkling lights become shining stars. Sparkling bands of garland transform into shimmering swaths of white diamonds draped across a frozen landscape. Echos of distant laughter, we are skating and sledding by the pale light of a winter moon. The moonlight guides us through deep and intoxicating forests of balsam and pine, and leads us safely home. In the stillness and in the silence we hear Spirit whisper. Our hearts are filled with love, and we remember what we know to be true; we are Spirit at our essence.

Peace, hope, love, and joy, all found simply by being still. Winter in many ways may be harsh, but it is a perfect time for quiet reflection, and it is the ideal time for us to embrace solitude.

Today more than ever we need to remember to take some time to be still. A few peaceful moments in a quiet place is one of the best gifts we can give ourselves. If we can escape all the noise that surrounds us it will be easier to silence the incessant chatter within our minds. When we allow ourselves a quiet place and a little time to turn inward we can then listen to our higher self speak.

Our inner wisdom knows that we are missing out on all the beauty of the present when our thoughts are consistently someplace else. When we learn to be more present in the moment our relationships and our life experiences are bound to become richer and more meaningful. We know that our thoughts are intricately linked to our physical and mental well-being. The better control we have over our thoughts, the more control we will have over our overall wellness.

The ability to give our undivided attention to anything is essentially a matter of focus. Training our mind to remain centered on one particular thing also requires a bit of practice. One way of improving our ability to concentrate and to be present in the moment is through meditation.

## The Best Present

There are a number of different ways to meditate and there are literally thousands of different meditation exercises. Finding an exercise that resonates well with you should not be a difficult task. Taking a class that offers guided meditations could definitely be beneficial, but it is not imperative. Simple, mindful practices that require nothing other than a few minutes of our time can be an ideal starting point. We can practice being present in the moment even as we go about our everyday activities.

The Christmas season may not seem like the right time to be adding something new to our already long list of things to do, yet, in actuality, it is the perfect time to start meditating. By taking a moment to center our full attention on the task at hand, we can experience a fragment of peace even amongst all of the chaos. Additionally, with a little focused effort we can find wisps of joy even in the most mundane tasks. Eating, drinking, shopping, traveling to work, or walking the dog, these are all great opportunities for us to practice mindfulness; all great places to discover a pebble or two of joy.

When we ask ourselves this question: "what am I doing at this very moment?", our mind will immediately direct us to the present as it naturally responds to the question posed. For instance, if we are walking the dog we can focus on each amazing step that we are taking. We will notice the strength in our legs and feel the firmness of the ground under our feet. With mindfulness we become more aware of the freedom of movement that we otherwise take for granted. We will hear the crunch of snow beneath our steps, and we will feel the crisp air filling our lungs. Suddenly we are feeling, sensing and experiencing the moment. We are turning an ordinary, everyday occurrence into a mindful experience.

No matter how busy the day or the season, whenever we feel that our mind is being pulled in too many directions we can always take a moment to regroup. A moment to be still. A moment to take three slow, deep breaths. We breath in calm and we exhale chaos. We breath in peace, we exhale disorder. We breath in hope, we exhale doubt. Even in the very depths of winter, out of nowhere, a little oasis of tranquility will appear. The more we practice being present in the moment the more we will be able to hear the gentle voice of our inner wisdom. When it asks us to be mindful, we will listen. When it asks us to be still, we will honor its request.

The art of being completely present in the moment is an invaluable skill that is definitely worth developing. Initially it does take a certain amount of conscious effort and commitment, but the end result is that everyone benefits. In a fast paced, multitasking, ever changing world this kind of presence is not easy. We may not be able to eliminate all distractions, but even minimizing them can be advantageous. Today more than ever we need to remember to take some time to just be. We seem to be in constant communication with someone, but often times we are failing to really be present. Undoubtedly, we can all appreciate how disappointing it is to look forward to visiting with a family member or friend, only to have them persistently distracted by some palm held gadget. On the contrary, how wonderful and refreshing it is when we can give each other our undivided attention. Whether it be for Christmas, or any other special occasion, instead of spending an inordinate amount of time and energy searching for that perfect gift to give to someone, we would do well to remember that it is our presence, body, mind and spirit that is by far the more valuable gift.

The week that is nestled between Christmas Day and New Year's Day is one of my favorite weeks of the year. There is something about this particular week that naturally invites us to take pause and be still. Standing on the precipice between the year that is almost past and the new one yet to come allows us a unique perspective. This vantage point beckons us to look forward, and to look back. We can see what worked well for us and we can take note of what did not. It is a perfect opportunity to envision the changes we would like to see and to be infused with the resolve needed to do things differently. Perhaps one resolution we can make for the new year is to be happier and healthier. With mindful practices that help us to be present in each moment, I believe we can indeed succeed.

..........................

Years ago, despite times being much simpler, people still gravitated toward nature for inspiration and reprieve. Before the Christmas tree became a popular household tradition, during the winter solstice, ancient people would bring evergreen boughs into the home as a reminder of all that would grow again when summer would return.

While glistening snowflakes fall all around us in hushed silence, beneath the white velvet, tiny seedlings patiently wait for the promise of spring. They do not doubt that soon enough sunshine will gently greet them, and that life will begin anew. For the present, they know they must be still. For now, they will simply have to be.

Chapter 13

# Mirror Mirror

*If you wish to see a new reflection
you will have to change more than
just the mirror.*

Suddenly, it's springtime! Yeah! A blessing of inspiration. The season when passion and promise collide. Everywhere we turn, an explosion of colour, fresh and vibrant. Everything is being roused from a long winter's slumber. The difference in the air is palpable. Something is stirring within us, and outside of us. We cannot necessarily see it, but we sense that it is the innate energy of spring.

More than just a strong desire, we feel an inherent need to bring the outdoors in. We open the nearest window, allowing the fresh spring breeze to enter. Immediately, it begins to work its magic. We may, or may not see the movement, but we can most certainly sense the change. Fresh air replaces the stagnant, breathing in deeply, we too feel refreshed and invigorated. Out with the old and in with the new.

Looking about, perhaps it's clear to us that we need to freshen more than just the air. Over time our home will provide us with a surprising sketch of who we are, and allow us an uncanny glimpse into the state of our present day lives. If we feel that the image we are looking at is no longer fitting or desirable, we are going to have to change more than just the mirror to see a new reflection.

Springtime provides so many wonderful opportunities to readily experience, and thereby understand the effect that our surroundings have on us. Whether it be the colourful displays of spring blossoms appearing at the supermarket, or witnessing the very first crocuses peeking up through the snow, these telltale signs of spring never fail to uplift us. Similarly, we can recreate these springtime feelings of joy by surrounding ourselves with all that we love most. This does not have to be an expensive process. With a little creativity, and by keeping an open mind, we can enhance just about any inhabitable space, and make it feel more like our own. No matter how great or humble our abode, if it doesn't quite feel like our castle, then applying some basic principles of feng shui could be to our advantage.

Feng shui in its simplest form, as described by R.D. Chin in *Feng Shui Revealed*, "is the practice of placing or arranging objects within a space so that they are not only pleasing to us, but also naturally support us within the context of that space."

Because everything we bring into our dwelling vibrates at a different frequency, we benefit immensely when our belongings and surroundings resonate in such a way that they help balance and uplift us. The colour of a room, the placement of furniture, and the articles displayed will all affect the flow of energy, determining our level of comfort in any given space. Some of us may be more sensitive to this energy than others, but we will all experience the effects of the vibrations emanating from every person, place, or object.

Feng shui is a multidimensional art. It is about the movement of energy and how that flow can be altered to benefit us. It is about colour and texture, shapes and substance. Rich with symbolism and full of practicality, feng shui is exciting to learn and fun to apply.

We can implement feng shui in various ways, however, ideally we should begin by first assessing our living space. This is done with the use of an ancient tool called a ba-gua. A ba-gua is basically an octagon with eight sections and a center. Each section represents a different aspect of our life. The sections include: career, knowledge, family, wealth, fame, marriage, creativity, and helpful people. Using our ba-gua like a map, we then superimpose it over the space at hand. With the room divided into nine areas we can see that each section of the room corresponds to a specific area of our life. We can then try to balance and enhance the energy within each space. By doing this we will affect, and improve the equivalent part of our life.

To put this into context, the entrance to our home is designated as our career center. Imagine it in constant disarray. We misplace our keys, trip over the shoes lying askew, step on a wet puddle of flooring and leave the house irritated and running late. The tone is set for the rest of the day. We are on a perpetual roll of rushing, followed by frustration. We may have physically closed the door on all the disorder in our entrance way, but the emotional chaos that we left the house with continues to follow us throughout our workday. We return home exhausted, and the first thing to greet us is the same mess we left behind at the start of the day.

Now let's apply some practical feng shui magic. We lay out an inviting welcoming mat, and move the pile of shoes to a rack in the closet. We place a unique bowl on the entrance table for keys, and we replace the dying plant with a lovely bouquet of our favourite flowers. A noticeable difference can be both seen and felt immediately. We can now leave for work organized, on time, and with a smile on our face. Consequently, our workday reflects this. We return home happy, and are happy to return home. Not really magic, just common sense mixed with a little flair!

Despite feng shui's growing popularity in the West, I had not heard of the term until a few years ago. My introduction to this ancient Chinese art came about in a rather unusual way.

Two things that I have purposely tried to steer clear of over the years are night shifts and tabloid papers. Given my choice of career however, neither are entirely avoidable.

One night, while watching over a confused patient, I couldn't help but notice a sensationalized headline in a paper that happened to be lying there at his bedside. In huge bold lettering it stated something to the effect of, "Hang a Mirror and Become a Millionaire." Definitely an attention grabber. With the patient asleep and nothing to do other than watch his bedcovers rhythmically rise and fall, I proceeded to read further. Just as I finished the first paragraph, a colleague stopped by, glanced at the headline, and emphatically exclaimed, "How ridiculous!" Not to be dissuaded, I simply waited for her departure and then continued reading. Despite the initial exaggerated claim, the article turned out to be an enlightening introduction into the fascinating world of feng shui.

Have you ever initially judged someone or something to be utterly ridiculous, only to later discover the hidden gem in what you had prematurely dismissed? Thankfully, not only does the Universe offer us an abundance of choices, it also graciously allows us the privilege to change our opinions.

Fortunately, I did not dismiss the article as quickly as my colleague did. Instead, by being curious and by keeping an open mind, I was both entertained, and thoroughly intrigued. Craving more knowledge, the next few months were spent reading through every book that the local library had on the subject of feng shui. With many different schools of thought being practiced, there were some conflicting views, but the general principles resonated well with me.

Our dwelling is essentially an extension of ourselves. Our aim should be to create a nicely balanced atmosphere that feels comfortable, and supports the direction of our lives and our aspirations. After evaluating the layout of each space in our home we might be delighted to discover that we intuitively managed to have arranged each room such that the energy in the room flows smoothy, and all is balanced harmoniously. However, should we not feel comfortable or uplifted in any given space, applying a few feng shui fundamentals is certainly worth considering. One might be surprised to find that a positive difference can be created simply by adjusting the arrangement of a few pieces of furniture or decorative objects.

Maybe it is the color of the room itself that we are not in balance with. A new coat of paint in a hue that inspires us, and harmonizes well with the area of focus, can be transformational. If that isn't feasible, making a conscious effort to freshen and de-clutter any room or closet is an inexpensive and effective way to improve the feel and flow of energy. By keeping only the stuff that we truly need and love, and by donating our excess, we will feel lighter and happier. By doing this we are not only helping ourselves, but others who are less fortunate might benefit as well.

Feng shui is a wonderful combination of ancient wisdom combined with the fanciful. Ultimately, I believe its purpose has always been to help us live in harmony with our surrounding environment. It stands to reason that anything designed to improve our health, wealth, and happiness, is worth consideration.

Eventually, I did buy a comprehensive book to keep for ongoing reference. Interestingly enough, when I went to renew the last lend on feng shui from the library, the book was mysteriously no longer in their catalogued system. The librarian then asked me if I would like to keep the book. Gratefully, I accepted. Now I have a second feng shui book to enjoy. Just another wonderful example of the Law of Attraction in action.

Did I instantly become a millionaire by hanging the perfect mirror in my entranceway? Not exactly. However, I do believe that life is a reflection of our beliefs. If we truly believe in abundance, then it will become our reality. Hmmm! Perhaps, the mirror did work after all.

## Chapter 14
# Small Things Do Make a Big Difference

> "Let us always meet each other
> with a smile, for the smile is the
> beginning of love."
>
> MOTHER TERESA

*S*imple stories. Often they can be the most memorable. This wonderful Japanese folktale sums up perfectly how life reflects what we put out back to us.

> Long ago in a small, far away village, there was a place known as the House of 1000 Mirrors. A small, happy little dog learned of this place and decided to visit. When he arrived, he bounced happily up the stairs to the doorway of the house. He looked

*through the doorway with his ears lifted high and his tail wagging as fast as it could. To his great surprise, he found himself staring at 1000 other happy little dogs with their tails wagging just as fast as his. He smiled a great smile, and was answered with 1000 great smiles just as warm and friendly. As he left the House, he thought to himself, "This is a wonderful place. I will come back and visit it often."*

*In this same village, another little dog, who was not quite as happy as the first one, decided to visit the house. He slowly climbed the stairs and hung his head low as he looked into the door. When he saw the 1000 unfriendly looking dogs staring back at him, he growled at them and was horrified to see 1000 little dogs growling back at him. As he left, he thought to himself, "That is a horrible place, and I will never go back there again.*

It doesn't take a great deal of effort, nor does it cost us a thing, yet what an enormous difference a little smile can make. We can convey so much without the help of a single word, for even the slightest upturn of the lips can speak volumes.

When we get caught up in our own thoughts, we are sometimes unaware of our facial expressions. Because first impressions can make lasting

## Small Things Do Make a Big Difference

impressions, it helps to be mindful of what we are silently saying. With a gentle smile, we can express both kindness and confidence, which are both extremely beneficial to the receiver, as well as to the provider. The presence of a genuine smile can improve just about any situation, but when our lives are placed in the hands of another, a smile can make a world of difference.

Years ago, following a hospital restructuring, I found myself working the most challenging surgical unit of my career. The specialty services that we provided were many and varied. Most of the patients that we cared for were either in need of, or had just undergone, a radical and life altering operation. Inevitably, the attention that they required was either intensive, time consuming, or both.

Despite my best efforts there never seemed to be enough time to provide the level of care that everyone deserved. Against all odds I was still determined to try. In the process I often wore myself out both physically and emotionally. I don't imagine I smiled very much during that time. I also knew that eventually I would likely have to pay a price for all that added stress. Indeed, I was not mistaken. When I left that unit it was with an added back injury, and one less organ. Fortunately it was one I could live without.

## Pebbles of Joy

To be a caregiver, rather than the one needing the care, is a gift for which I have always been grateful. I never would have expected a role reversal to be advantageous, but much to my surprise, it turned out to be a real blessing. From a patient's perspective, it was quite an enlightening experience for me to discover just how invaluable a smile could be. With every interaction I found myself immediately feeling safe and trusting, or tense and uncertain, the only difference being the presence of a friendly smile.

While waiting to undergo surgery it is not uncommon to worry about the "what ifs." What if I don't wake up? What if something goes wrong? What if the pain is unbearable? I thought about none of these things.

I woke up. Nothing had gone wrong. The pain was tolerable. What would have been a seven to ten day stay in hospital a decade earlier was now just a day surgery. I would be home in a few short hours, albeit, less a gallbladder.

As I prepared to leave, a conversation with a patient that I had recently cared for came to my mind. He was recovering from major surgery. Along with multiple intravenous lines, he had tubes sprouting out from just about everywhere. Several bags were collecting a variety of different coloured fluids. Dressings

## Small Things Do Make a Big Difference

covered him front and back. I was worried! I also had five other patients to look after. Most of them were in a similar state. Did I mention I was worried? My concern was not a lack of knowledge or skill to safely care for everyone; my fear was finding the time to effectively do so. Was I smiling? No, I was not.

"You're scaring me." Those were the first words he said to me. I felt awful. As if he didn't already have enough to fret about? When I asked him "why," he answered, "Because you look so serious. I'm afraid that means something is wrong."

Now I understood. I had experienced first hand what a big difference a little smile can make.

I carried this pearl with me the remainder of my career. Greeting every new patient with a smile was a must. Sometimes it was difficult to maintain when a patient's condition turned dire. I may not have always succeeded, but I always did my best to camouflage my fears for them with confidence and compassion. A soft voice and a gentle smile would invariably be reassuring, creating a remarkable difference in an otherwise tension charged atmosphere. When the crisis was over, the patient would often not remember everything that had transpired. What they did recall, and would convey much gratitude for, was the kindness of the caregivers.

## Pebbles of Joy

Yes, a smile can be very powerful. We can express kindness with words or without. A warm hug, a hot cup of tea, a heartfelt compliment, a listening ear, the possibilities are infinite. Whatever we choose, if it comes from the heart and is offered with a smile, it will help to elevate our collective level of joy. Small things do make a big difference!

The old saying, "The mouth speaks what the heart is full of" may date back to biblical times, but the truth within remains.

Today, we live in a world that places enormous emphasis on beauty and fashion, but, of course, not everyone can measure up to society's standards of perfection. Nevertheless, we must remember that a smiling face will always appear more youthful and attractive, and that kindness never goes out of style. A genuine smile welcomes us to look beyond all outward appearances and to truly see what the heart has to offer.

Just in case you happened to skip by the opening quotation for this chapter, it's worth repeating here: "Let us always meet each other with a smile, for the smile is the beginning of love." If a happy little dog can figure this out, surely there is hope for the rest of us.

Chapter 15

# Finding Love

"Love is patient and kind."

1 CORINTHIANS 13:4

*I* tend to smile a great deal more these days. In part, because I believe in the Law of Attraction, and partly because of something I thought I didn't want.

My husband had wanted a puppy for a long time. I did not. For me, having a dog was synonymous with more work. Something I absolutely did not need. So my response was consistently some variation of "Not now!" Eventually, my husband either got tired of waiting, or tired of my excuses. Now we have a happy little dog. Correction, make that two happy little dogs!

Sometimes what seems like a bad idea is just

the opposite. Indeed, I was not mistaken about the extra work. That turned out to be even more than I had anticipated. The resulting smiles, laughter, and love however, now that is something I could never have imagined.

It used to be a mystery to me how we never seem to be able find love when we are desperately searching for it, but love always has a way of finding us whenever we selflessly give it away. Finally, thanks to my husband, and two lovable puppies, I'm beginning to understand.

Buddy was the first to arrive on the scene. Fluffy, cuddly, gentle, and adorable. It was definitely love at first sight. Then came Sophie a little over a year later. One afternoon I arrived home from work to a furry little surprise. She was safely tucked up against Buddy's protective chest. Clearly Buddy found her to be irresistible. Unfortunately, I did not. With a mangy black coat and long black claws, I could immediately see that grooming was going to be a real problem. In addition, she had way too many teeth for her tiny mouth and a very noticeable underbite, causing several of them to be on continuous display. Quite frankly, she looked more like a miniature gremlin than a puppy. Sadly, I wasn't immediately feeling the love.

## Finding Love

Although I had a few initial concerns regarding Sophie's condition, I never could have imagined the extent of her problems. Initially I did not know that it would take me years to find something that would freshen her very bad breath. I also did not realize that her incessant scratching and hair loss was due to a microscopic skin mite. The word microscopic may give the impression that the issue was tiny, but I assure you, those mites were a huge inconvenience. She was vulnerable to ear infections, and would also require treatment for a nasty parasitic bowel infection. Lastly, because of her dislocating knee caps and questionable vision she would need to be carried up and down most flights of stairs. Incredibly, all of these challenges surfaced before or just after her very first birthday. And yet, long before that day and in spite of all these difficulties, I loved her more than I ever thought possible.

This unexpected love may seem impossible. Clearly none of Sophie's problems can be considered endearing. If you factor in my obsession with cleanliness and combine it with an aversion to anything creepy crawly, common sense would dictate that this could only be a recipe for disaster, not love. Yet therein lies the difference between our limited vision and God's creative genius.

Reaching far beyond our fears and prejudices we embrace compassion and allow our hearts to expand. There is never a shortage of love as long as we are allowing it in and then sending it back out. This is our magnificent connection to our loving Creator and to every other living thing. Sometimes it just takes a little Sophie to remind us that love really is limitless and that it is only our thoughts that cause us to believe otherwise.

We come from a place of pure love and our Spirit knows only pure love. Consequently, a life without love just doesn't make much sense to us. Love is the creative power by which our world expands. Love creates the masterpiece: a lovely garden, beautiful music, and an inspiring story. It is love that heals the wounded, and love that creates another living being.

There is definitely no shortage of love in our world. Thinking otherwise is really just an illusion, an illusion that will send us on a desperate search for something we are not likely to find, because searching for love will only keep us searching for love.

If our experience is one of constantly wondering why there appears to be a lack of love in our lives, we must remember that love works on the same principle as the Law of Attraction. What we are giving out is what will be reflected back to us. As long as we are thinking about lack, we will continue to experience more lack. Whether it be health, wealth, or love, the rules never change. Thinking thoughts of scarcity will keep us trapped in scarcity.

We have to think and believe in abundance. There really is an unlimited supply of love within us as well as all around us. Sometimes, we need to be reminded that it may not manifest as the perfect package that we were expecting. Within every one of us is a sacred breath of life called our Spirit. If we open up our hearts and look through the eyes of that Spirit, we can be sure to recognize love in a multitude of disguises.

Every now and then a movie stays with us long after the credits have been played. For me, Shallow Hal was one of these movies. It was directed by the Farrelly brothers and released in 2001 by 20th Century Fox. Although classified as a romantic comedy, I believe it was so much more than just that. In the movie, Shallow Hal is searching for love. True to his name, he doesn't settle for anything less than physical perfection. Not surprisingly, love eludes him. With the promise of finding his dream girl, he agrees to be hypnotized. Consequently, he sees everyone's inner radiance manifested as physical beauty.

When the spell wears off, he is shocked to discover that his new found love looks nothing like he imagined. Fortunately, love has transformed him. Shallow Hal is now a much deeper and wiser Hal, and in the end, true love prevails.

Imagine being able to see the beauty and goodness in others upon meeting them. If our first thought is, "Wouldn't that be a wonderful gift to have?", our very next thought should be, "Wait a minute, we do possess that ability." We practice it every time we combine loving kindness with intuition. When we stop viewing the world through the eyes of fear, judgement, and distain, and instead choose to look with kindness and compassion, we'll see genuine beauty and love everywhere.

I gave up searching for love a long time ago, and yet my life is now full of love. Looking at my little Sophie, all I see is a beautiful and loving puppy. Love, like happiness comes from within. It is not out there somewhere, hidden and elusive. It is found within us, flowing like water from its God given source. We send it out into the world, and it comes back to us, multiplied.

May all the love you are wishing for, and dreaming of, find its way through you, and back to you.

## Chapter 16
# Three Wishes

*Sometimes we just need to let go and be free; have fun, be childlike, wish upon falling stars and candles on a cake.*

If someone was to grant you three wishes, what would you wish for? Would it be for world peace? An end to hunger? Abundance for all? With unlimited options to consider, it really isn't easy to choose.

No matter how many times I play this game with family or friends, the answers given never fail to amaze me. Sometimes, to make the task more specific and indulgent, I change the rules. For instance, the three wishes now become one, and it must be something you would want specifically for yourself.

Now, what might you wish for? I imagine that love, money, and health, would top the list. However, if you already have all three, then perhaps what is missing is the time to enjoy your blessings.

So, do we wish for more time, or to be more discerning with how we use it? How many of us have heard some version of the saying, "no one on their deathbed lies there wishing that they had spent more time at the office?" We all wholeheartedly agree, yet we proceed to carry on status quo.

Have we outsmarted ourselves by creating a world where everything must run at maximum efficiency? To keep up, must we too follow at the same speed? The day is always going to be just twenty-four hours long. Not shorter, not longer, but time is relative and it's up to us to find a way to slow it down.

Anyone that has ever cared for a young child is likely familiar with the famous words, "Time Out!" but when was the last time you assigned the same reprieve for yourself?

Remembering the importance of taking time for oneself is good, but it isn't very useful unless you actually follow through with it. Many will argue that there is never enough time for such an indulgence, and I am here to remind you that, whether you think there is, or you think there isn't, either way you will be right.

Sometimes I have to wonder if we are so distracted by our busy and hectic lives that we don't even realize that we are gradually forgetting how to relax and have fun: the kind of pure enjoyment that costs little more than our time. Then again, perhaps the problem isn't so much that we are forgetting how to effectively unwind, but rather, we are not remembering how important it is to our well-being.

Because the Universe often uses unconventional methods of teaching, some of our most valuable life lessons will not be gleaned from textbooks or classrooms. This might explain why, despite spending an inordinate amount of time studying throughout high school, the lesson that resonates clearest in my mind is one that my younger brother inadvertently taught me.

You might think that he would have been dissuaded by the stack of books in front of me, but every night, like a hopeful and patient puppy, he would sit with me at our old kitchen table anticipating the moment the last notebook closed. Strangely enough, I don't remember him ever having any homework of his own. Perhaps he had more lenient teachers, possibly lighter courses, or maybe

I should just buck up and admit that he was always a lot smarter than I. Regardless, every evening, spring through fall, his mission was to engage me in a game of volleyball, soccer, or both. Too often I resisted. However, his persistence always paid off and we would invariably end up playing many more rounds than I ever initially agreed to.

Back then I don't imagine that either one of us could have appreciated the importance of balancing work and play. Likewise, we never had to think about getting enough exercise. To a farm kid, that would be the equivalent of wondering if we were getting enough air. Truthfully, once the snow had melted and the grass had turned green, we were just grateful to receive a brand new fully inflated ball. Then, fortunately for both of us, Wally made sure it was not going to sit idle for long.

To this day, coming across a colourful display of globe sized balls instantly sends me catapulting back in time. I don't think about any of the school work that I spent hours cramming into my brain. It may have been important at the time, but it isn't now. Instead, I recall the smile on my brother's face when he finally persuaded me to play. I hear our shouts and our laughter. I relive those carefree moments when tumbling onto cool grass was done

## Three Wishes

on purpose, simply because it was such a refreshing contrast to the warm evening air. Sometimes on clear nights we would lie there staring up into the darkening sky just waiting to wish upon that first falling star.

Do I recall what I wished for? Of course not. Do I still remember to look up at the night sky and dream? Absolutely! City lights may have dimmed the view but the celestial beauty and mystery remain ever vibrant in my mind.

When you can't sleep at night, step outdoors and look up into the midnight sky. Just for a moment, let time stand still and allow the heavens to reveal to you some of their long held secrets.

As I have mentioned before, the Universe is friendly, and it is in constant communication with us. It speaks in any number of ways, but it's up to us to pay attention and listen carefully to understand what it is patiently trying to teach us.

These days, I seldom need persuading to head outdoors and enjoy all that nature has to offer. When inclement weather would otherwise succeed in deterring me, I now have two small dogs that have faithfully taken up my brother's torch.

One of the very first lessons my little dog Buddy was quick to remind me of was how to be healthier and happier by working less and playing more. In his world, there is never any excuse good enough to take priority over exercise and play time. On the other hand, although she enjoys a good run, little Sophie's area of expertise is definitely relaxing. Her directive is simplicity at its finest. Claim a sunbeam and take a nap.

Pets can be such an inspiration to us, if we only take the time to appreciate the wisdom in their prompting. Yes, they can be quite expensive, but the way they fill our lives with richness is magical.

Understandably, everyone's situation is unique. As years come and go, our commitments, finances, and health will change. Sometimes these changes will be extreme. However, some of the best indulgences do not require a great deal of time, stamina, or money. The simplest things can still recharge us with much needed energy and joy. For instance, spending a few moments outdoors watching the sun come up can be extremely pleasurable and restorative. Immersing oneself in that quiet space before the world wakes up is a type of meditation exercise that just about anyone can do and benefit from. Despite the rewards, an extrovert might consider this kind of quiet time to be the epitome of boredom. Instead, gathering with a group of friends for a favorite sport might be far more engaging and rejuvenating. These impromptu activities need not cost much at all. Apart from our time, the only expense is the price of the required ball.

I believe we all know what we need both physically and mentally to feel more joyful and free. We just need to start listening to, and honoring, that inner voice that always knows what's best for us.

Wherever we are along the continuum of life, there may be things that we wish we had done differently. We may wish that we had worked less, that we had enjoyed more time with family and friends, or that we had spent less time worrying and more time doing. Without a doubt, worry, like fear, can significantly diminish our enjoyment of life. On the other hand, a good sense of humor can do the opposite. I imagine we can all relate to Mark Twain's famous words, "I have been through some terrible things in my life, some of which actually happened." Hopefully we too can see the humor in our own folly. Twain also reminds us to embrace the spirit of fun and adventure with the following statement, "Twenty years from now you will be more disappointed by the things you didn't do than by the ones that you did do. So throw off the bowlines. Sail away from the safe harbor. Catch the trade winds in your sails. Explore. Dream. Discover."

No matter how many or how few moments we wish we could change, there is no going back in time. Regardless of the number of years that have slipped by, it may not be too late to start or finish something we should have done long ago. We may not be able to change the past, but we can still influence the future. We can begin by asking ourselves this question, "What is it that we truly wish for?" When we have the answer to that question, then the Universe will help us make that wish come true.

When I was actively nursing I often wished I could heal with a simple touch. Although I was adept at making people comfortable, there were times when adequate pain control was not possible. After exhausting every available measure, I would often declare, "I wish I had a magic wand to instantly make you feel better, but I do not. Sometimes, we just have to place our trust in the tincture of time." With the words "this too shall pass" eventually whatever "it" was, did.

Time has a way of healing many things but we must remember to use it wisely. Sometimes we need to use our time to laugh and play. Other times, we simply need to rest and be still.

## Chapter 17
# A Time For Change

> "Not all of us can do great things, but
> we can do small things with great love."
> MOTHER TERESA

*I* believe that at some point in our lives we all question the meaning of life. Within these moments of contemplation, I imagine we ask ourselves some variation of the following questions: "Am I living a life of purpose? Is there something different or more meaningful I should be doing with the time I have left? How much time do I have left? Will it be enough for me to do all that I was meant to do?"

These are profound queries, the answers to which may not easily be forthcoming. So, to simplify, we could ask ourselves the following: "Am I living up to my potential, or is there a dream clamoring within me that I am not honoring?" If we are honest with ourselves, we should be able to answer both parts of that question with a straight forward, yes or no.

Of course, that's the easy part. How we respond to that initial prompt will determine if we need to ponder the second, more complex question: "Why am I not choosing to be all that I wish to be, why am I not following my heart's true passion?" Now here is where you might be inclined to defend your position should it be less than ideal. However, no matter what you may think to the contrary, we do have a choice in all that we do. We do have a choice of what we can become. Our dreams do not abide within us to taunt and to torment, but instead they are there to motivate and uplift us. We just have to believe!

If a persistent little voice tries to dissuade you from following your dreams, claiming that there isn't a way, remember the quotation at the very beginning of this book, "Everything is possible for the one who believes." These words, spoken by Jesus, remind us that there is always a way! To begin, we must stop dwelling on all the excuses supporting why we "can't," and start focusing on all the reasons why we "can."

## A Time For Change

Without a doubt, experience can be our finest teacher. Although we learn from our successes, we probably learn more from our so called failures. We might wish to totally forget our colossal blunders, but, they do serve as a great reminder of what not to do. A good memory should serve us well.

Sometimes the greatest obstacle preventing us from reaching our potential is our past. Despite having no form or substance, our memories seem to possess a superpower all of their own. Some have the extraordinary ability to knock us down just as surely as if we had collided with a brick wall. Others might keep us running the longest marathon imaginable as we desperately try to escape the phantoms of our past. Indeed, sometimes memories can be quite the impressive illusionists.

It never ceases to amaze me how we can latch onto the most hurtful and insensitive comment or deed, then assign it more merit than any compliment or kindness thereafter. We have to ask ourselves, "How much did I miss out on because I allowed one moment of a distant yesterday to colour all of my todays?" We should never permit anything or anyone to wield so much power over us. If someone once told you that you are not good enough, it can only become true if you choose to believe it. Instead, you must realize and honour the truth. You are far more than just good enough. If you're having trouble believing me, consider the following: imagine a loving Deity creating any one of us, than saying, "Hmm, not quite good enough. Oh well, too bad for you. Next!" I don't think so! No matter what anyone says to the contrary, we must remember that we really are good enough. We are absolutely perfect for the role we were meant to play in this lifetime.

Sometimes there's just no making sense of things done out of anger or ignorance. Whatever the transgression may be, we must find a way to let it go. There is absolutely no point in chaining ourselves to heartache of the past, and then dragging it along like a cement block. Letting go of memories that serve no useful purpose is like clearing clutter. Get rid of what you do not want, and surround yourself with all that inspires you.

Whenever you decide to take a trip down memory lane, make sure it's a good one. Focus on and be grateful for the experiences that uplift you, do not linger on those that make you feel diminished. Remember, the only real power the past has over us is what we give it. Prior experiences may influence our future, but they absolutely do not determine it. Our strength lies in the present. The very thoughts we are having right now are the ones affecting the remainder of our story.

A whole new panorama opens up before us when we realize that the quality of our human experience is affected more by what is going on within us than by what is occurring around us. Taking responsibility for where we are in life is not the same as blaming or criticizing ourselves for what may be a less than favourable situation. Instead, it is a major step toward self-empowerment, and a window through which we can view freedom: the freedom to change things for the better, and the freedom to be all that we were meant to be.

Depending on our unique situation, and what we are trying to accomplish, sometimes our options will be severely limited. Still, we are always free to choose our attitude and our thoughts. For instance, the time may come when we are no longer able to even feed ourselves, and yet, we can still nourish another with kindness, with wisdom, and with our generosity of spirit.

If we are transitioning from one stage of life to another, and are in need of insight and inspiration, *Man's Search for Meaning*, by Viktor Frankl, is a read worth considering. In view of all that he had witnessed during his many years in a concentration camp, Frankl determined that, "everything can be taken from a man but one thing: the last of human freedoms-to choose one's attitude in any given set of circumstances, to choose one's own way." He also reminds us, "When we are no longer able to change a situation . . . we are challenged to change ourselves."

Life is synonymous with change. Day turns to night, summer to winter. We grow older. Ideally, we grow wiser. Our purpose is constantly evolving. Living up to our potential might require a change to occur within ourselves. Sometimes we foolishly resist, thinking that this entails giving up an important part of who we are. The opposite, however, is true. Our Spirit is entirely aware of our magnificence even if we are not. It is continuously leading us back to our authentic selves so that we might achieve all that it knows we are capable of.

Staying true to ourselves is crucial to our happiness, our success, and our well-being. A glacier etching through the landscape will leave a mark. Similarly, our life experiences are going to shape us. However, they do not define us. If ever we feel that outside forces are carving us into something that we would rather not be, then it's time to return to our center. It's time to revisit our core values and beliefs, to get reacquainted with our authentic self. By retreating into silence we allow our inner voice of wisdom to be heard. It will help us rediscover who we truly are, that is, our authentic self. What we feel with the most passion will lead us to where we need to be.

In *The Master Key System*, Charles F. Haanel states, "If you wish to change conditions you must change yourself." In his text he includes a wonderful all encompassing affirmation. It was sent to him by a young man who created it as a means to heal from what was said to be incurable. Ten powerful words replace all thoughts of fear, lack, and limitation, with courage, power, self-reliance, and confidence. They are, "I am, whole, perfect, strong, powerful, loving, harmonious, and happy." These are words reminding us of our magnificence. If we were to commit this to memory, and truly believe it, imagine what an enormous difference this could make in our lives.

As our planet revolves around the sun, the seasons change. The earth spins on its axis and darkness turns to light. From where we stand we cannot see the movement, but we do experience the results. Each action causing a reaction. When enough of our thoughts have turned from fear to love, and from negative to positive, we are bound to experience our world differently.

Suddenly, we are not just wishing on the stars, we are reaching for them. No longer are we constantly ambushed by fear. We can finally envision our dreams becoming reality. We feel supported by the Universe, and it responds in kind.

Some say the sole purpose of life is simply to be happy. I can't tell you with any degree of certainty whether that is true or not. Although I believe happiness is essential, I also believe that there is far more to this life of ours. When we are genuinely happy, life does seem to have more purpose, but at the same time, the more meaningful our lives, the happier we feel. Given that there is a clear and definite connection between the two, we can trust that our internal guidance system will always let us know if we are heading in the right direction and doing what we were meant to do. If we are on course, we should feel a comfortable balance to our lives, a genuine feeling that all is well, and yes, we should easily be able to say, "I am happy."

We know that we are eternal, but this incarnation is not without an undisclosed expiry date. As we move along this particular finite continuum, we feel that invisible clock ticking. Every now and then the chimes sound, reminding us that it is time. Time to move on. Time to move forward. Time to give back. Time for something different. Time to make a difference. One day we wake, and we just know, it is time for us to begin a new chapter.

Our lives are stories unfolding, great adventures resounding with excitement, drama and fun. We have all written our own script, and therefore understand best what it is we need to accomplish. You are no exception. Look beyond the moment and decide whether what you see reflects what you truly want and believe in. Reach for what is good and meaningful. Take some risks. Believe in yourself. Believe in a loving Creator. Do not let a day go by undiscovered. Know that your path is not that of another. Wake with passion and with purpose. Be grateful for each day, and always hope, and aim for the best.

## Chapter 18
# Some Things are Not Meant to Disappear

> "Whenever we begin to feel as if we can no longer go on, hope whispers in our ear, to remind us, 'we are strong'."
>
> ROBERT M. HENSEL

*H*ope. It is such a little word, until you attempt to define it. Far more than just a wish or a desire, hope is really all encompassing. We are constantly hoping for something. Sometimes for small things, and at other times for great things. We hope for a sunny day, and we hope for world peace. Sometimes we are filled with hope and at other times we feel that we have lost all hope. Where does it come from, and where does it go? Why do we have it and how do we lose it?

Hope isn't just wishful thinking, it is something far more powerful. I believe hope is our intimate connection with the Divine. We will feel the most hopeful when we are experiencing a close connection and we feel the most bereft when we disconnect emotionally. When we wander off our chosen course we simply lose the frequency or signal that our well-being is dependent on.

Remember that our personal story is created through our thoughts and feelings. Because hope is such a deep feeling, firmly connecting us with the Divine, it is essentially what allows us to both entertain, and to believe in infinite possibilities. Not only is hope the initial spark that ignites the passion within us, it is also the current of energy that helps to propel us forward.

Hope is a thought, that like a seed, needs time to grow. It only makes sense that faith and trust are the feelings we need before we see any results. We hope for plenty of sunshine, but we expect that there will also be rainy days. All are part of the growth process. Sometimes we will experience deluges that wash away all that we carefully planned, planted, and nurtured. No matter how much faith and trust we have, some seeds were never meant to flourish, perhaps because room was needed for something else to grow.

Most of us experience times in our life where we are pummeled by one too many storms. Feeling too tired to continue to struggle against the current, we might eventually find ourselves adrift on a very big ocean with nothing safe or familiar in sight. With daylight fading, so are our hopes. At this point we are probably feeling totally abandoned and forgotten. Then, just as we are about to be completely engulfed by darkness, we see a tiny speck of light in the distance. This is hope! That perpetual glimmer, just waiting to help guide us through the night.

We can be certain that hope cannot be completely extinguished. When we think it lost, it is only our thoughts that have misplaced it. When we think that we have been abandoned, it is only our pattern of thinking that has caused us to feel separate. Without hope we will feel contracted, with hope we will always feel expanded, like the canvas catching that first gust of wind and setting our sail in motion.

We may be a great distance away from having our feet planted securely on dry land, but as intimidating as this vast expanse of ocean surrounding us may seem, it is precisely what is keeping us afloat. Whether we fear and curse it or love and embrace it, the Universe is always there to support us. How we experience that will be determined by our thoughts.

Life is a journey with boundless paths available for us to take. With so many directions to choose from, and all kinds of weather to endure, is it any wonder that sometimes we wander or drift off course? However, just as we know that the sun is always shining beyond the clouds, we can be sure that hope is constantly available to us. When we happen to glance in the right direction, we will catch a glimpse of that sunbeam, and with the wind at our back, we will make our way home safely.

There is no denying hope plays a huge role in everyone's life. It may be a natural part of our every day thinking process, but unless we are feeling a certain level of desperation, we don't consciously give hope a great deal of thought. Despite its direct effect on our well-being, including a chapter on hope was something that I had not initially considered. To compensate for my oversight, the Universe had to intervene.

It may seem peculiar, but sometimes we do

lose touch with some of our closest friends. Then one day out of the blue, regardless of the number of years that have elapsed, our paths collide. Not by coincidence, but by a magnificently orchestrated Universe that brings us together as we align our thoughts. Clearly, for some time, Carolyn and I had simply been thinking of each other. Although I had not seen my dear friend in almost a decade, all of a sudden in the most unlikely place, there she was sitting right in front of me. Like the angels of long ago, Carolyn would be the ideal messenger to ensure that a chapter on hope would not be overlooked. Even though she has weathered more than her fair share of intense storms and personal loss, Carolyn is always full of hope.

Our friends, family members and pets are going to drift in and out of our lives like the ebb and flow of the tides. Although the cycle of life is a natural part of the human experience, often it is one that many people will struggle with the most. Carolyn and I tend to view this cycle through a shared lens. The colour of that lens is hope.

Life is precious and fragile. Sometimes, it can also be ever so fleeting. Naturally we want to hold onto it as long as humanly possible. Hope allows us to let go. When our loved ones pass it is natural for us to feel lost. Unable to see beyond the veil that we are separated by we might stare blindly into an abyss. Hope turns us around. It knows that we will not find our loved ones in darkness, but rather, in light. Our fears may prevent us from remembering that we are eternal, but hope ensures we do not forget.

Indeed, hope is many things. Hope is power, and it is love. It is sunshine and kindness. Hope lifts us up out of nowhere, and brings us back together. It is dismissing doubt, and choosing to believe. Hope is our gateway to possibilities. It is knowing that anything is possible, and that a possibility is probable. Hope is moving forward, without fearing what has past, or what may come. Hope is a glimpse into the future; to see the master plan, the blueprint completed. It is appreciating the entire tapestry, and trusting in each others' part. Hope is a gift to enchant us into continuing on with our life story. It is what keeps us believing in happy endings, and it is the sacred bond that brings us home safely.

Chapter 19

# A Never Ending Story

> "You are not a human being in
> search of a spiritual experience, you are a spirit
> immersed in a human experience."
> 
> TEILHARD DE CHARDIN

We are eternal, we are loved, and we are one. Once we believe that, we are well on our way to creating the life that we were meant to live. A life where peace and joy, no longer elusive, become our ever faithful companions.

I believe that we have all chosen to incarnate here on this planet so that we could grow in love. In spirit form we chose our parents, our family, and our friends. We planned an agenda and lessons that we would complete, and we knew that when our time was up, once again we would in spirit form return home.

## Pebbles of Joy

When we know exactly where we want to go in life, it stands to reason that it will be a lot easier for us to get there. On the contrary, if we have no particular destination in mind, or we forget where we are going, chances are greater that we will wander aimlessly, often times ending up in the same position in which we started.

Having said that, it is a bit of a mystery that when we arrive on this earth plane we seem to have no clear recollection of any of our carefully laid plans. No longer are we certain of the correct path, the direction in which we are meant to travel, or even the actual purpose of our trip.

Seriously, who would voluntarily sign up for such an unpredictable adventure? There would have had to be more to the agreement. Well, of course, we are not going completely unprepared. Whether we choose to believe it or not, a loving Creator will always be with us. We will have our own personal support system, made up of angels, guardians, and spirit guides available on call twenty-four hours a day, seven days a week. We will also be equipped with a no-fail internal compass, otherwise known as intuition. Programmed to always point us in the right direction, this guidance system will not let us down. However, we must remember that this inner voice of

## A Never Ending Story

wisdom can only be helpful if we listen to it and trust in it. Lastly, throughout this adventure we will be able to create the type of life we wish to experience by virtue of our thoughts and our feelings.

Well, now we're talking! Sign me up! Then we arrive here on this strange planet, a vulnerable, fragile infant, and what is the first thing we do? We start to cry. Maybe it's because we forget everything, and therefore think that we are lost. Maybe we remember too much, and desperately want to go back. Perhaps, a little of both.

So what do we do? Hopefully, the best we can. We work through our lessons one by one, sometimes excelling at them, sometimes repeating them. At times we travel the main road together, some days we take the path less trodden, and journey on our own, eventually, one way or another, making our way back home.

In the end we will ask ourselves: "Did we accomplish what we set out to do? Did we transcend our fears, or live within them diminished? Were we courageous enough to bask in the sunshine and embrace the spirit of adventure, or did we hide in the shadows, too frightened to take a risk?"

Finally, we will have to face and answer the most important question of all: which wolf did we choose as our ever faithful companion?